Warcraft™ II

Tides of Darkness

The Official Strategy Guide

NOW AVAILABLE FROM PRIMA

Computer Game Books

The 11th Hour: The Official Strategy Guide
The 7th Guest: The Official Strategy Guide
Ascendancy: The Official Strategy Guide
Blackthorne: The Official Strategy Guide
Celtic Tales: Balor of the Evil Eye—The Official Strategy Guide
Cyberia: The Official Strategy Guide
Descent: The Official Strategy Guide
DOOM Battlebook
DOOM II: The Official Strategy Guide
Dragon Lore: The Official Strategy Guide
Dungeon Master II: The Legend of Skullkeep—The Official Strategy Guide
Frankenstein: Through the Eyes of the Monster—The Official Strategy Guide
Hell: A Cyberpunk Thriller—The Official Strategy Guide
Heretic: The Official Strategy Guide
I Have No Mouth and I Must Scream: The Official Strategy Guide
In The 1st Degree: The Official Strategy Guide
The Journeyman Project 2: Buried in Time—The Official Strategy Guide
Kingdom: The Far Reaches—The Official Strategy Guide
King's Quest VII: The Unauthorized Strategy Guide
Lords of Midnight: The Official Strategy Guide
Marathon: The Official Strategy Guide
Mech Warrior 2: The Official Strategy Guide
Microsoft Space Simulator: The Official Strategy Guide
Myst: The Official Strategy Guide, Revised Edition
Oregon Trail II: The Official Strategy Guide
Prisoner of Ice: The Official Strategy Guide
Romance of the Three Kingdoms IV: Wall of Fire—The Official Strategy Guide
Shannara: The Official Strategy Guide
Sid Meier's Colonization: The Official Strategy Guide
SimCity 2000: Power, Politics, and Planning
SimEarth: The Official Strategy Guide
Terry Pratchett's Discworld: The Official Strategy Guide
Thunderscape: The Official Strategy Guide
TIE Fighter: The Official Strategy Guide
WarCraft: Orcs & Humans Official Secrets & Solutions
Warlords II Deluxe: The Official Strategy Guide
X-COM Terror From The Deep: The Official Strategy Guide
X-COM UFO Defense: The Official Strategy Guide

How to Order:

For information on quantity discounts contact the publisher: Prima Publishing, P.O. Box 1260BK, Rocklin, CA 95677-1260; (916) 632-4400. On your letterhead include information concerning the intended use of the books and the number of books you wish to purchase. For individual orders, turn to the back of the book for more information.

Warcraft™ II

Tides of Darkness

The Official Strategy Guide

Ed Dille
Eric Anthony Morman

PRIMA PUBLISHING

Artwork provided by Samwise Didier, Roman Kenney, Chris Metzen, Micky Neilson, Stuart Rose, Ron Millar, Dave Berggren, Brian Sousa, Duane Stinnett, Nick Carpenter, Trevor Jacobs, Collin Murray, Matt Samia, and Eric Flannum, all of Blizzard Entertainment.

Project Editor: Daniel J. Francisco

ISBN: 0-7615-0188-6
Library of Congress Catalog Card Number: 95-72236
Printed in the United States of America
96 97 98 99 BB 10 9 8 7 6

To all the programmers, artists, writers, designers, and producers of video games, whose talents have provided more than twenty years of digital entertainment. Some are better than others, but all have helped gaming evolve into its own art form.

Contents

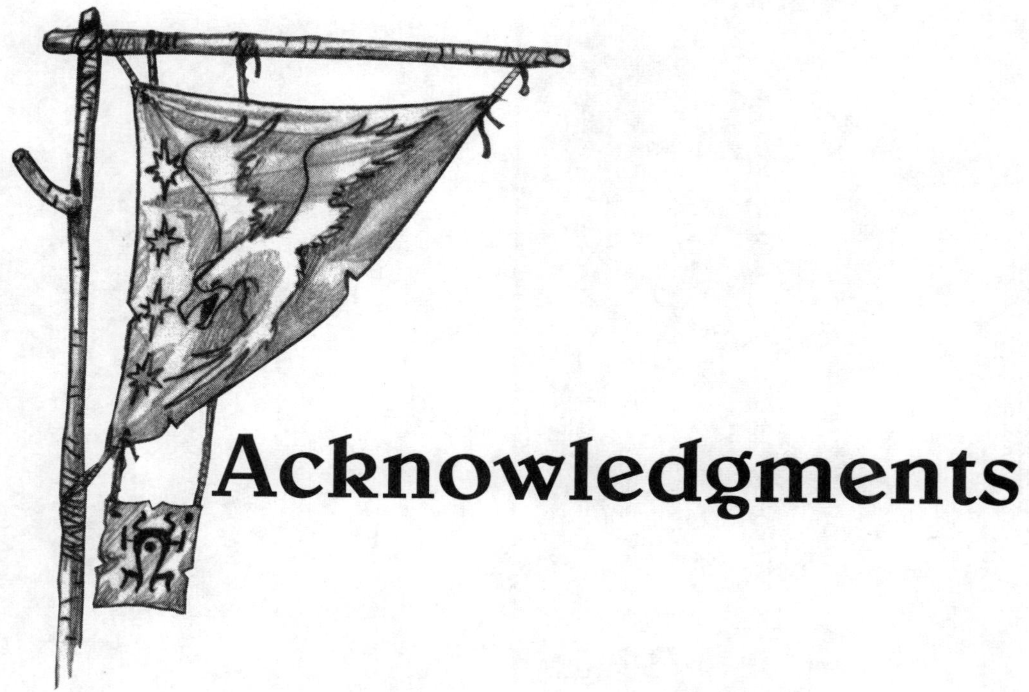

Acknowledgments

First, I would like to thank Bill Roper and the entire gang at Blizzard Entertainment for providing invaluable information and original art, all of which made this book extraordinary.

More thanks go to Andy Swann here at Fog Studios, who worked many long nights and days off on this project. Without his help, we would not have the detailed mission maps, which were no simple task to compile.

Finally, the efforts of Dan Francisco at Prima Publishing and stunning layout by Marian Hartsough must be recognized for molding a stack of words, numbers, and pictures into a beautiful finished product. It was a privilege to work with them, and I look forward to future projects with the entire crew at Prima.

Tony Morman
Wolf Creek
December 1995

Acknowledgments

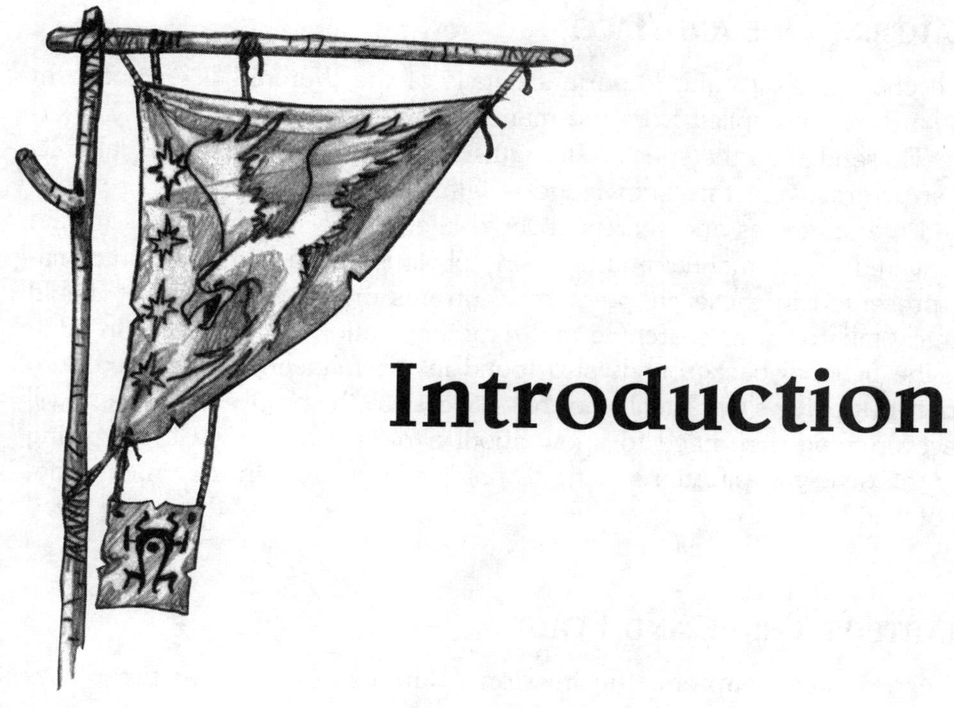

Introduction

How to Use This Book

A lot of creative effort went into the making of Warcraft II, and even hardened war game veterans will find it a challenge, hence the need for this strategy guide. During the fast-paced struggle for survival against friends or the enhanced computer artificial intelligence, many important details get overlooked, shrouded by random factors that continually change the outcome of battles. This book is designed as a quick reference for vital information, an invaluable source of strategic tactics, and a compliment to the rich fictional background that enhances the flavor of the game.

Chapters One and Two

These chapters cover the important details of the Warcraft II environment with hard data compiled from the manual, game, and editor for easy reference. These identify the specific strengths and weaknesses of individual units and structures, and this knowledge is vital to understanding the reasons behind the strategies and secrets covered later. Since topics such as terrain are covered in the manual and are fairly obvious in the game, the information presented in these chapters concentrates on the minutia that would normally take a lot of searching and experimentation to ferret out. In addition, the fictional backgrounds also found in the manual are repeated here for network players who might not have access to them. Overall, players will have everything they need to know about a particular item, without giving away the deadly applications of these predictable factors in the chaotic theater of war.

Chapters Three and Four

In the next two chapters, the mission solutions assume that the player already has a basic understanding of the game. For example, it is given that one must constantly produce workers and farms to provide reinforcements in missions that do not have a fixed number of units to work with. Exactly when or where to make these additions is difficult to define because of constant setbacks from losing units and structures to enemy attacks. Having a large labor pool increases the chances of building up adequate defenses, but there is no guarantee of success with the unpredictable nature of the game. Furthermore, certain strategies that produce consistent results from one mission to the next are referred to only briefly after a description in the first applicable situation. Therefore, it is suggested that players start reading from the beginning of the chapter if a method seems unclear in later scenarios.

It is important to remember that the Horde and Alliance missions follow separate paths in the same timeline. For example, in the first Warcraft game, the Human missions ended with the defeat of the Orcs and the restoration of lasting peace in Azeroth. Warcraft II, however, is based on the assumption that the Orcs were ultimately victorious in the first game, and the struggle for survival begins again six years after the relocation of the Human survivors to a new continent. During this time, the Orcs and their allies have been constantly pouring through the Portal and have laid waste to the lands around it. Hence, they need to spread their nihilistic plague to foreign lands for the simple reason that food for their livestock cannot grow on scorched and barren earth. Choosing command of the Horde continues the Orcs' conquest of the world, while taking up the noble cause of the Alliance rewrites history in its favor. Players will notice that several Horde and Alliance missions take place on the same soil, but commanding one side or the other determines which army emerges victorious on that particular battleground.

Since there are many different methods of completing a mission, the solutions herein represent the simplest and most direct application of overwhelming force to obvious weaknesses in enemy defenses. As the number of new units and spells increases, so does the time and effort required to produce them, not to mention the trouble of having to select an individual unit to cast an enchantment. Speed and efficiency usually produce the best and most consistent results, so the solutions generally involve the use of basic units in large numbers. For example, the development and use of Death Knights in the Horde solutions is not necessary when a more conventional approach is just as effective; hence, they are not mentioned after they become available. Choosing to use them can only increase the chances of success, and allows players to develop unique uses for their talents as they see fit. Therefore, the clever application of all the spells and unconventional methods is saved for last.

Chapter Five

The final chapter contains a wealth of previously undocumented tips, tactics, and secrets that describe the effective use of combined knowledge in specific situations. These are the tools with which to gain the upper hand against both computer and human adversaries, but their use requires an intimate knowledge of the game to know when to apply them. Both the Alliance and Horde armies are well-balanced against each other, and the cheat codes affect all players when enabled, so the key to mastering Warcraft II lies in the ability to recognize hidden weaknesses and exploit them as efficiently as possible.

Reaching this level of expertise would normally require weeks of game play and experimentation, but the advice given here will greatly speed this process.

The first section of the final chapter details the standard tactics applied in the mission solutions to clarify exactly why those methods are universally effective in nearly any battle. These are also very useful in network wars where players may not have time to build advanced structures and units before enemies start pouring in from all directions. The next section covers dirty tricks and traps, listed in random order because many of them fall under several different topics at once. This also allows players to learn only as much as they want at any given time without giving away every little secret in the game at a glance. Readers of this section are encouraged to pick only a few hints, then experiment to learn their specific applications before moving on. Finally, the dreaded Cheat Codes are listed at the end of the book. They should only be used as a last and desperate resort to situations that simply cannot be overcome otherwise. These tend to make the game too easy, but be warned that they benefit all players when activated, even the computer to a limited degree.

Conclusion

The information in this book follows a logical progression from basic truths to comprehensive strategies, allowing players to work upward from any skill level, novice to veteran. Those not wishing to ruin the fun of developing their own solutions can find the answer to a specific problem and close the book to continue; others may want to know as much as possible to decimate their opponents, and reading from cover to cover will certainly enable them to do so.

Additionally, every effort was made to preserve the fantasy setting of Lordaeron with prose from the manual and original accounts of events from the perspectives of both armies. Much more than just a hint book, these pages open a window to another world, and reveal the dark secrets hidden within.

Warcraft™ II
Tides of Darkness
The Official Strategy Guide

METZEN - 95

Chapter One

Warcraft II Armies

"What is Steel,
compared to the Hand that wields it?"

—Thulsa Doom, *Conan the Barbarian*

From lowly workers to elite spellcasters, the might of any army is judged by the quality as well as the number of its soldiers. Placing a weapon in someone's hands does not make them a worthy opponent if it is not used properly. This chapter describes all the talents and shortcomings of every combatant on both sides of the war.

Alliance Units

Peasant

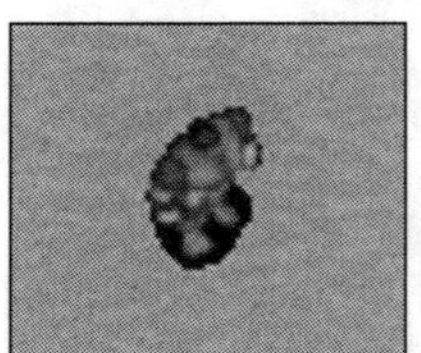

Visual Range:	4
Hit Points:	30
Magic Points:	–
Build Time:	45
Gold:	400
Lumber:	–
Oil:	–
Attack Range:	1
Armor:	–
Basic Damage:	3
Piercing Damage:	2
Effective Damage:	1–5
Speed:	10

Peasants are trained from the hard-working and stout-hearted citizens that live in the numerous kingdoms of Lordaeron. Because they mine gold and harvest lumber to meet the ever-increasing needs of the fighting force that must push back the unrelenting Horde, they are the backbone of the Alliance. Trained in the construction and maintenance not only of the myriad buildings found in every community, but also of those necessary to wage war, they take great pride in the invaluable service they provide. Roused by tales of the Orcish atrocities in Azeroth, these Peasants have learned to use both pick and axe for their own defense if threatened.

FOOTMAN

Visual Range:	4
Hit Points:	60
Magic Points:	–
Build Time:	60
Gold:	600
Lumber:	–
Oil:	–
Attack Range:	1
Armor:	2
Basic Damage:	6
Piercing Damage:	3
Effective Damage:	2–9
Speed:	10

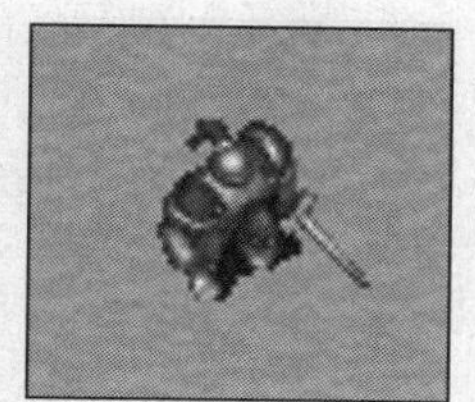

Footmen are the initial line of defense against the Horde. Arrayed in hardened steel armor, they courageously wield broadsword and shield in hand-to-hand combat against their vile Orcish foes. Footmen are ever prepared to heed the call to arms, joining the throng who do battle.

Elven Archer

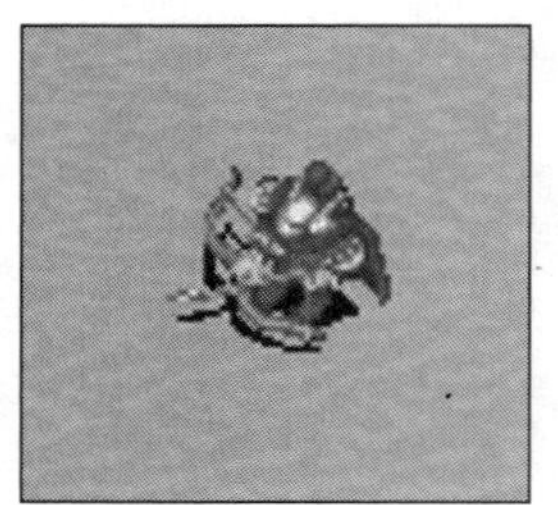

Visual Range:	5
Hit Points:	40
Magic Points:	–
Build Time:	70
Gold:	500
Lumber:	50
Oil:	–
Attack Range:	4
Armor:	0
Basic Damage:	3
Piercing Damage:	6
Effective Damage:	3–9
Speed:	10

Out of the mysterious forests of Quel'thalas come the Elven Archers to aid the Alliance in its darkest hour. Descendants of the elder race of Lordaeron, these agile woodsmen are unmatched in their use of the bow. Unencumbered by helmet or heavy armor, Archers are keen of eye and fleet of foot. These Elves have long been embroiled in a bloody conflict with the hated Trolls of Lordaeron, and are quick to loose a rain of arrows on any foe.

Elven Ranger

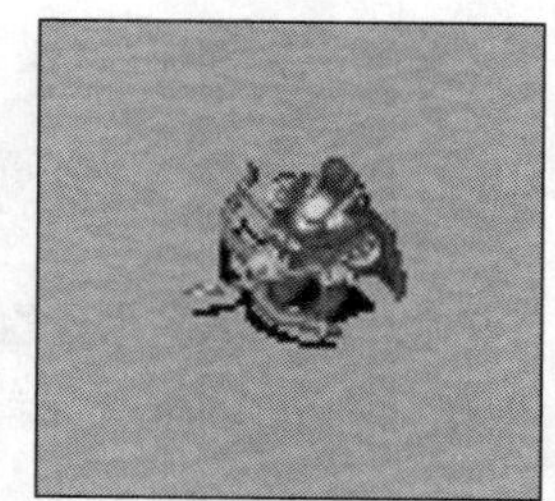

Visual Range:	6
Hit Points:	50
Magic Points:	–
Build Time:	70
Gold:	500
Lumber:	50
Oil:	–
Attack Range:	4
Armor:	0
Basic Damage:	3
Piercing Damage:	6
Effective Damage:	3–9
Speed:	10

Rangers are a special cadre of Elven Archers who are intimately bound to the wildlands of Lordaeron. Their pursuit of mastery in Longbow, Marksmanship, and Scouting makes them more rugged and even deadlier than their brothers; owing to these traits, they are greatly feared by their enemies. These secretive elite warriors have never involved themselves in the affairs of Humans, but when Horde onslaughts threatened to destroy the Elven homelands, they quickly offered their services to the Alliance. Although their numbers are few, their presence can change the course of the war if they are deployed wisely.

Knight

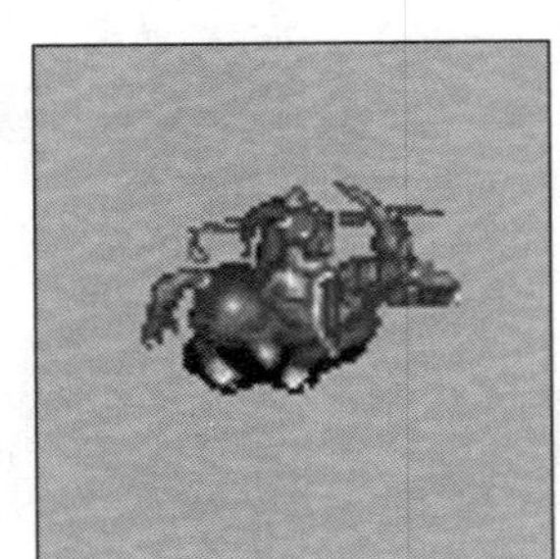

Visual Range:	4
Hit Points:	90
Magic Points:	–
Build Time:	90
Gold:	800
Lumber:	100
Oil:	–
Attack Range:	1
Armor:	4
Basic Damage:	8
Piercing Damage:	4
Effective Damage:	2–12
Speed:	13

The Knights of Lordaeron represent the fiercest fighting force in the armies of the Alliance. Protected by suits of heavy armor, they carry mighty warhammers to crush all who would threaten the freedom of their lands. Astride great warhorses, these honorable and just warriors symbolize order to the peoples of Lordaeron in these dark and chaotic times. Having learned of the fate suffered by the Knights of Azeroth after the First War, they have sworn both to avenge their fallen brethren and to free their homelands from the grip of the Orcish Hordes.

PALADIN

Visual Range:	5
Hit Points:	90
Magic Points:	255
Build Time:	90
Gold:	800
Lumber:	100
Oil:	–
Attack Range:	1
Armor:	4
Basic Damage:	8
Piercing Damage:	4
Effective Damage:	2–12
Speed:	13

Paladins are a holy order of warriors whose purpose is to defend and shepherd the war-torn populace of Lordaeron. The Archbishop Alonsus Faol perceived that the pious Clerics of Northshire, who suffered such terrible attrition in the First War, were ill prepared for the dangers of combat. Along with many of the surviving Clerics of Northshire, he sought only those of the greatest virtue among the knighthood of Lordaeron and tutored them in the ways of magic. It now falls to these Paladins—christened the Knights of the Silver Hand—to heal the wounds sustained in combat and to restore faith in the promise of freedom from Orcish tyranny.

Paladin Spells:

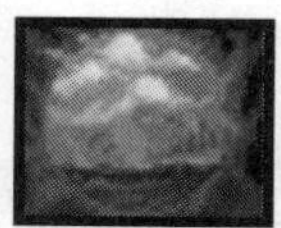

Holy Vision

Spell Point Cost: 70

Just as the spirit of Humankind is everywhere, so the Holy Vision of the Paladin extends to all corners of the land. When this incantation unveils an area to the Paladin, it also grants him knowledge of the terrain and of all those who may dwell within it. When this spell dims, the Paladin retains knowledge of the lands he has seen, although he loses sight of the denizens of these lands.

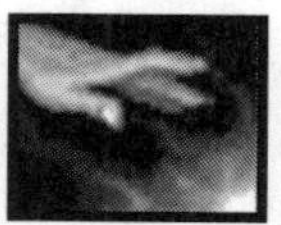

Healing

Spell Point Cost: 6 per 1 point healed

Aiding our brethren in times of pain and illness remains the fundamental concern of any within the holy order. By focusing his spiritual powers, the Paladin can heal those who have been wounded in battle. Although only one being at a time may be healed in this fashion, healing replenishes the strength and courage of all who strive for victory against the callous Orcs.

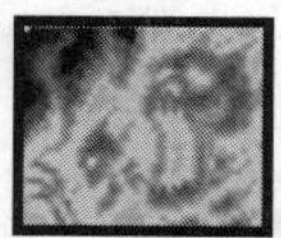

Exorcism

Spell Point Cost: 4 per point of damage

Calling on the forces of light and purity, the Paladin can dispel the walking dead that plague the lands of Azeroth. Exorcism can be used to cause injury to a group of these undead terrors, or to utterly eradicate a single one. These creatures of Hades seem to gain strength in numbers, so the greater the number of undead in a group that is being exorcised, the less actual damage each one will take. This act is extremely taxing for the Paladin, making it necessary for him to observe a period of rest before once again invoking this great power.

Ballista

Visual Range:	9
Hit Points:	110
Magic Points:	–
Build Time:	250
Gold:	900
Lumber:	300
Oil:	–
Attack Range:	8
Armor:	0
Basic Damage:	80
Piercing Damage:	0
Effective Damage:	25–80
Speed:	5

The Ballista launches steel-tipped bolts to impale all in their paths. Because an awesome amount of force must be exerted on their tremendous bowstrings, these machines of war are reinforced with lumber from the precious Ironwood trees. The Ballista, a product of Human design and Elven craftsmanship, symbolizes the unity of all who have allied themselves against the Horde. The Gnomes are also valuable allies, in that they may be employed to design improved missiles that make the Ballista the most devastating weapon of the Alliance.

MAGE

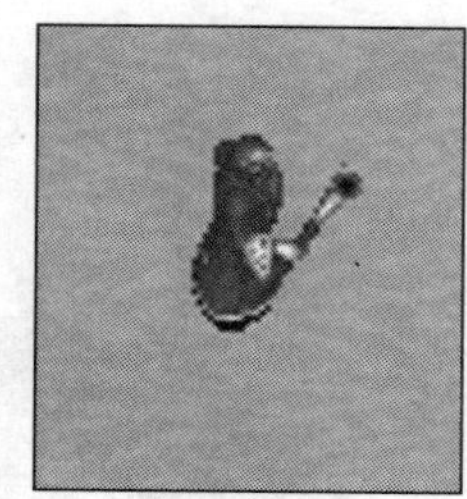

Visual Range:	9
Hit Points:	60
Magic Points:	255
Build Time:	120
Gold:	1,200
Lumber:	–
Oil:	–
Attack Range:	2
Armor:	0
Basic Damage:	0
Piercing Damage:	9
Effective Damage:	5–9
Speed:	8

Once students of the Conjurers of Azeroth, the members of this new order of Mages have been forced to discover untapped magical forces to command in their war against the ruthless Orcs. Although they were masters of their art, the Conjurers who fell during the First War were unprepared for the rigors of war. Determined to avoid a similar fate, the Mages have undertaken a regimen equally demanding for body and soul, thus dedicating themselves to the command of more aggressive and destructive magicks. Whether in their sanctum at the Violet Citadel in Dalaran or on the many battlefields of Lordaeron, the Mages are resolute in their efforts to defend the people.

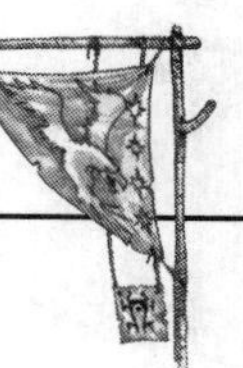

Mage Spells

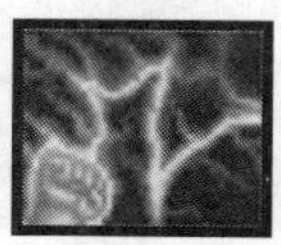

Lightning

The Mages of Lordaeron have the ability to discharge lightning from their hands when entering a melee. These swift bolts of energy strike their victim regardless of any armor he may wear.

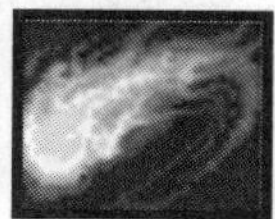

Fireball

Spell Point Cost: 100

Magicks involving the cardinal elements of the universe are favorites of the Mages. The Fireball is launched from the palms of the Mage and streaks like a blazing comet across the battlefield, slamming its fiery bulk into whatever stands in its path.

Slow

Spell Point Cost: 50

The Mages of Lordaeron have created a spell that hinders both movement and reflex. By warping the very patterns of time that surround the caster's target, Slow enables him to reduce an enemy's offensive to a crawl. Time cannot be held in check very long by even the mightiest of Mages, however, so the effects of this temporal shift cease as the power of the spell wanes.

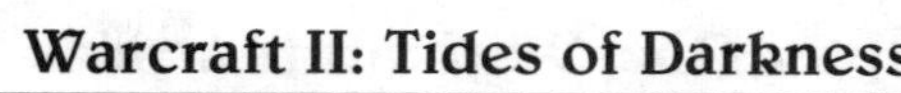

Flame Shield

Spell Point Cost: 80

Serving as both a weapon and a barrier, the Flame Shield is a binding of the chaotic force of fire to the aura of the Mage. A twisting helix of fire that whirls about the target, the Flame Shield accompanies the Mage wherever he may roam. Flame Shield will deliver damage to any enemy unit or structure it touches.

Invisibility

Spell Point Cost: 200

Gleaned from sacred tomes rescued from the debris of Northshire Abbey, this spell confers the ability to cloud the perceptions of others so that they cannot perceive the physical existence of the caster or his target. The individual who is rendered invisible may not perform any tasks, such as attacking, harvesting, or spellcasting. If he interacts with his environment in any fashion more aggressive than simple movement, his Invisibility will end; he will stand revealed.

Polymorph

Spell Point Cost: 200

Perhaps the most fearsome of the Mage spells, Polymorph alters the physical form of its target. This metamorphosis changes man to beast, forever warping both mind and body. This sorcery wholly transforms its victims into creatures of the wild, destroying their reasoning and thereby making commands for battle or for change of direction impossible.

Blizzard

Spell Point Cost: 25 per barrage

Summoning torrential storms from the frozen Mountains of Northeron, this potent spell calls down a fierce tempest of ice to assault the enemies of the Mage with its cold blades. Blizzard can be cast over large portions of the battlefield, so it is an extremely powerful spell for those facing legions of Orcish troops.

DWARVEN DEMOLITION SQUAD

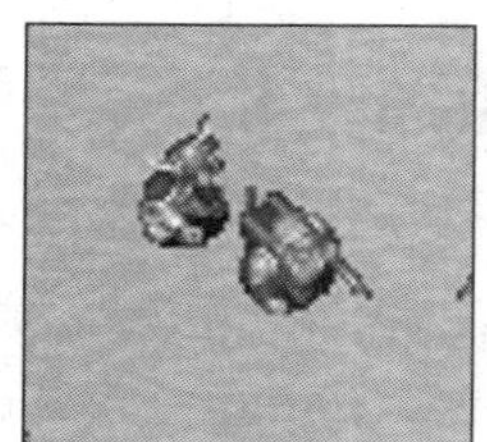

Visual Range:	4
Hit Points:	40
Magic Points:	–
Build Time:	200
Gold:	700
Lumber:	250
Oil:	–
Attack Range:	1
Armor:	0
Basic Damage:	4
Piercing Damage:	2
Effective Damage:	1–6
Explosive Damage:	400
Speed:	4

From the deep subterranean halls of Khaz Modan, the Dwarven Demolition Squad comes to aid the Alliance in its crusade for the liberation of Lordaeron. As masters of the handling and arming of explosives, the Demolition Squad is renowned for their ability to demolish any obstacle—from a mighty wall to a bulwark of solid stone. Reckless and bold, these Dwarves are zealous in their loyalty to the Alliance and would not hesitate to detonate their explosive devices if the situation turned grim.

Gnomish Flying Machine

Visual Range:	9
Hit Points:	150
Magic Points:	0
Build Time:	65
Gold:	500
Lumber:	100
Oil:	–
Attack Range:	–
Armor:	2
Basic Damage:	–
Piercing Damage:	–
Effective Damage:	–
Speed:	17

The Gnomes of Khaz Modan have long compensated for their lack of physical strength with ingenuity and daring. As members of the Alliance, they have continued to display their talents by inventing and piloting the astounding Flying Machine. Although their armor or armament is too light for them to serve as weapons of mass destruction, these awkward contraptions can be used to survey vast areas of terrain, making them invaluable for discovering the movements of the Horde.

Gryphon Rider

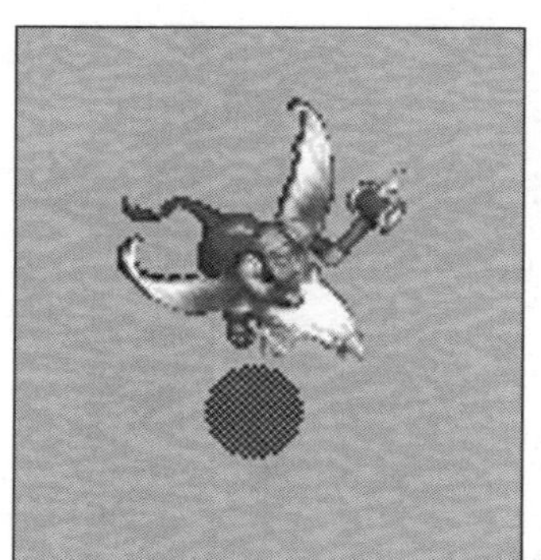

Visual Range:	6
Hit Points:	100
Magic Points:	–
Build Time:	250
Gold:	2,500
Lumber:	–
Oil:	–
Attack Range:	4
Armor:	5
Basic Damage:	0
Piercing Damage:	16
Effective Damage:	8–16
Speed:	14

From the ominous, threatening peaks of Northeron come the Dwarven Gryphon Riders. Mounted on their legendary beasts and wielding the mystic Stormhammers forged deep within the secret chambers of their Aviaries, these feral Dwarves fear no enemy—and rely on no friend. They have allied themselves only with the Elves of Quel'thalas, distrusting their Dwarven cousins and Humans alike. When the call to battle is sounded, however, they can be counted upon to fight alongside any who oppose the Horde.

Oil Tanker

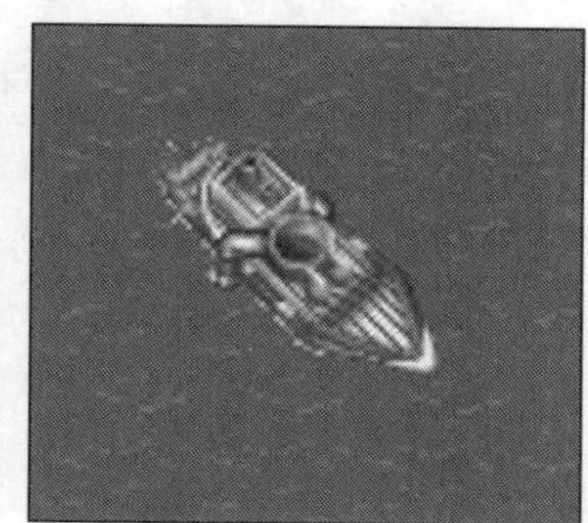

Visual Range:	4
Hit Points:	90
Magic Points:	–
Build Time:	50
Gold:	400
Lumber:	200
Oil:	–
Attack Range:	–
Armor:	10
Basic Damage:	–
Piercing Damage:	–
Effective Damage:	–
Speed:	10

Oil Tankers are the only ships that do not require oil for their construction. They are manned by hard-working, dependable mariners who search for the rich oil deposits that lie beneath the waves. The crew of every Tanker is skilled in building Oil Platforms and ferrying the oil back to a Shipyard or Oil Refinery where it may be processed and put to use.

Elven Destroyer

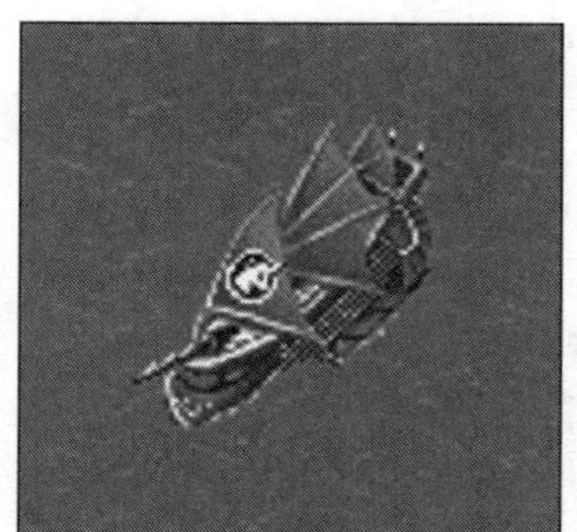

Visual Range:	8
Hit Points:	100
Magic Points:	0
Build Time:	90
Gold:	700
Lumber:	350
Oil:	700
Attack Range:	4
Armor:	10
Basic Damage:	35
Piercing Damage:	0
Effective Damage:	2–35
Speed:	10

Elven Destroyers are powerful warships from the fleets of Quel'thalas. Manned by highly skilled Elven seafarers, these swift vessels are prepared to engage the enemy wherever he may be found. Elven Destroyers constitute a critical part of the Alliance naval defense force.

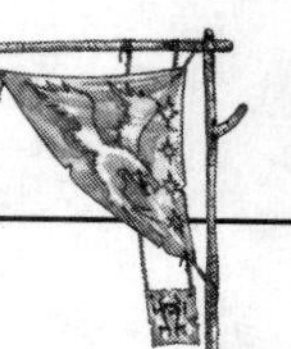

TRANSPORT

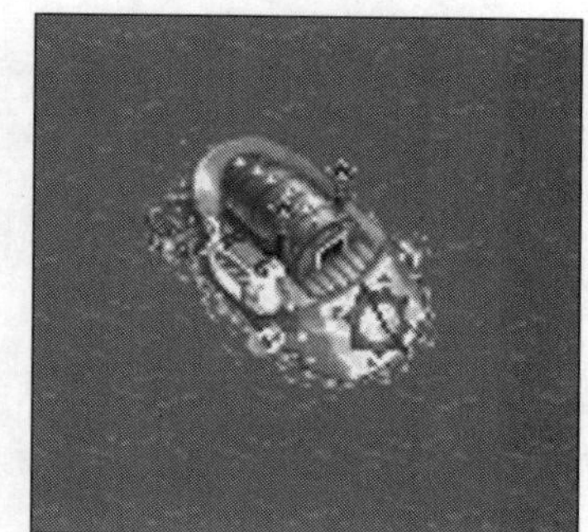

Visual Range:	4
Hit Points:	150
Magic Points:	–
Build Time:	70
Gold:	600
Lumber:	200
Oil:	500
Attack Range:	1
Armor:	0
Basic Damage:	–
Piercing Damage:	–
Effective Damage:	–
Speed:	10

Transports are a vital part of the Alliance war effort, for these sturdy vessels allow troops to traverse various waterways to engage in battle. Designed to carry and deliver several ground units directly onto the shore, Transports are slow and unarmed. Hence, they must rely on Destroyers and Battleships for protection.

Battleship

Visual Range:	8
Hit Points:	150
Magic Points:	–
Build Time:	140
Gold:	1,000
Lumber:	500
Oil:	1,000
Attack Range:	6
Armor:	15
Basic Damage:	130
Piercing Damage:	0
Effective Damage:	50–130
Speed:	6

The Alliance relies on its great Battleships to control the seas. These hulking behemoths possess armor and weaponry far greater than that of any other Alliance vessel. Their combination of devastating weaponry and substantial armor more than compensates for their somewhat sluggish speed in sea combat.

Gnomish Submarine

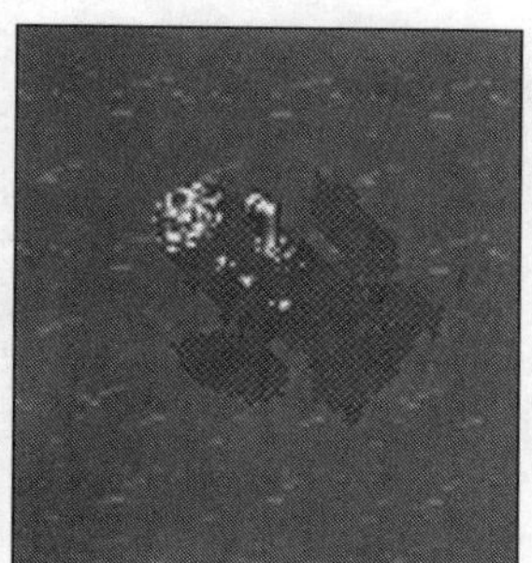

Visual Range:	5
Hit Points:	60
Magic Points:	–
Build Time:	100
Gold:	800
Lumber:	150
Oil:	900
Attack Range:	4
Armor:	0
Basic Damage:	50
Piercing Damage:	0
Effective Damage:	10–50
Speed:	7

The resourceful Gnomish Inventors have designed an amazing craft known as the Submarine. This watertight vessel can submerge itself beneath the waves and surreptitiously keep watch on enemy forces above the surface. The use of cunning and craft to carry out surprise attacks on more powerful enemies makes the Submarine an invaluable part of the Lordaeron armada.

UNITS OF THE ORCISH HORDE

PEON

Visual Range:	4
Hit Points:	30
Magic Points:	–
Build Time:	45
Gold:	400
Lumber:	–
Oil:	–
Attack Range:	1
Armor:	0
Basic Damage:	3
Piercing Damage:	2
Effective Damage:	1–5
Speed:	10

The label of Peon denotes the lowest station among those in the Orcish Horde. Deficient in all important skills, these inferior folk are assigned to menial tasks such as harvesting lumber and mining gold. Their labor is also required for the construction and maintenance of the buildings that support the vast undertakings of the Horde. Downtrodden, the Orc Peons slave thanklessly to please their overseers.

Grunt

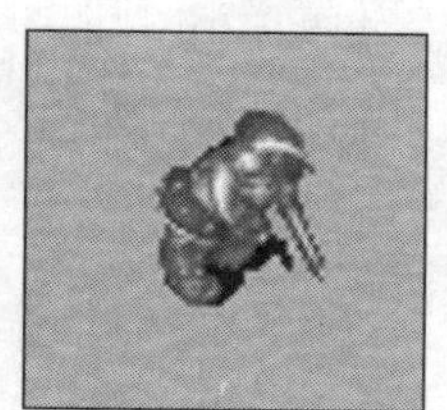

Visual Range:	4
Hit Points:	60
Magic Points:	–
Build Time:	60
Gold:	600
Lumber:	–
Oil:	–
Attack Range:	1
Armor:	2
Basic Damage:	6
Piercing Damage:	3
Effective Damage:	2–9
Speed:	10

Those Orcs who distinguish themselves sufficiently in the arts of war to be trained as Grunts epitomize the merciless spirit of the Horde. Equipped with mighty axes and battle-worn armor, they are prepared to fight to the death. Devoted to the Horde and to his clan, the Grunt lusts for battle, desiring only to wade into the field of carnage and die a bloody death surrounded by the bodies of his fallen enemies.

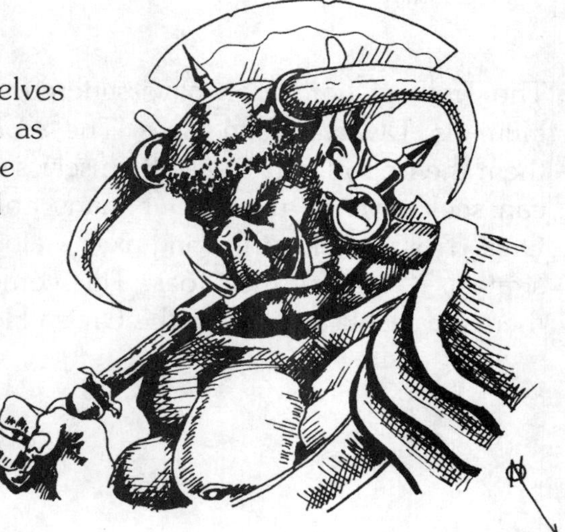

Troll Axethrower

Visual Range:	5
Hit Points:	40
Magic Points:	–
Build Time:	70
Gold:	500
Lumber:	50
Oil:	–
Attack Range:	4
Armor:	0
Basic Damage:	3
Piercing Damage:	6
Effective Damage:	3–9
Speed:	10

The Trolls of Lordaeron have suffered ages of attrition at the hands of the Humans, Dwarves, and Elves. The advent of the Orcish Horde has given them the opportunity to ally themselves with kindred spirits, with whom they can seek revenge upon their many enemies. More agile than the brutish Orcs, Trolls employ throwing axes—along with a cunning attack-and-retreat strategy—to assail their foes. This combination of speed and range makes them a valuable addition to the Orcish Horde.

Troll Berserker

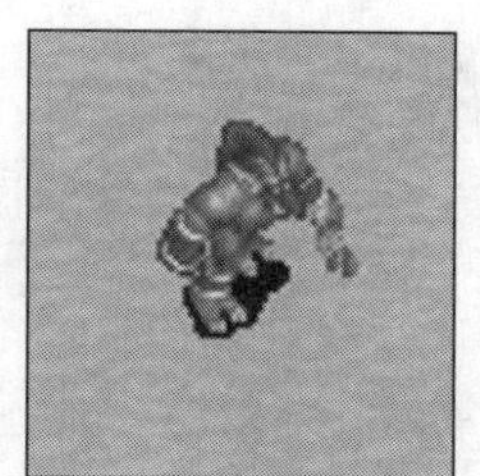

Visual Range:	6
Hit Points:	50
Magic Points:	–
Build Time:	70
Gold:	500
Lumber:	50
Oil:	–
Attack Range:	4
Armor:	0
Basic Damage:	3
Piercing Damage:	6
Effective Damage:	3–9
Speed:	10

Berserkers are a bloodthirsty sect of Trolls dedicated to the total annihilation of their hated enemies, the Elves. Having been subjected to numerous experiments with strange chemicals and potions by the Goblin Alchemists, the Berserkers have been given many strange abilities that make them all but unstoppable in the heat of battle. A Berserker may also enter into a battle-rage, which transforms him into a veritable cyclone of death and destruction.

Ogre

Visual Range:	4
Hit Points:	90
Magic Points:	0
Build Time:	90
Gold:	800
Lumber:	100
Oil:	0
Attack Range:	1
Armor:	4
Basic Damage:	8
Piercing Damage:	4
Effective Damage:	2–12
Speed:	13

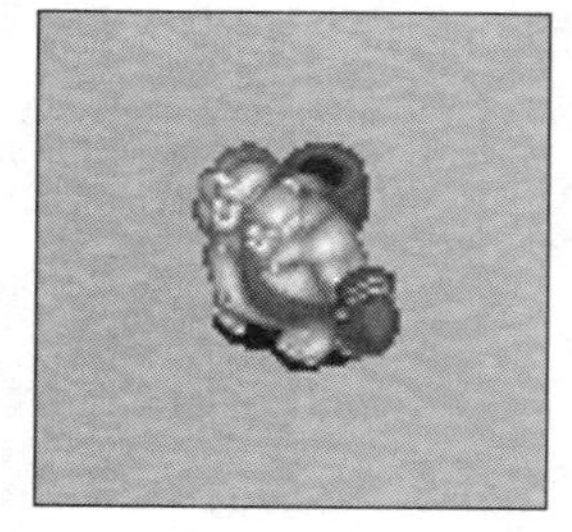

The Ogres are the monstrous two-headed allies of the Orcs that were brought through the Portal by the Warlock Gul'-dan after the First War. The Ogres act as enforcers in an effort to quell needless infighting between the Orc clans. Owing to the constant bickering between his two heads, an Ogre exhibits less intelligence than even the lowly Peon. The Ogres' enormous strength and unnatural toughness, however, place them among the fiercest warriors in the Horde.

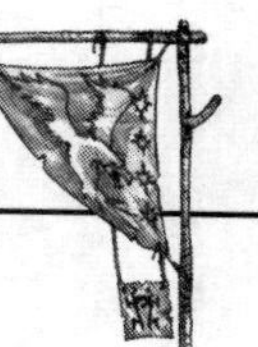

Ogre-Mage

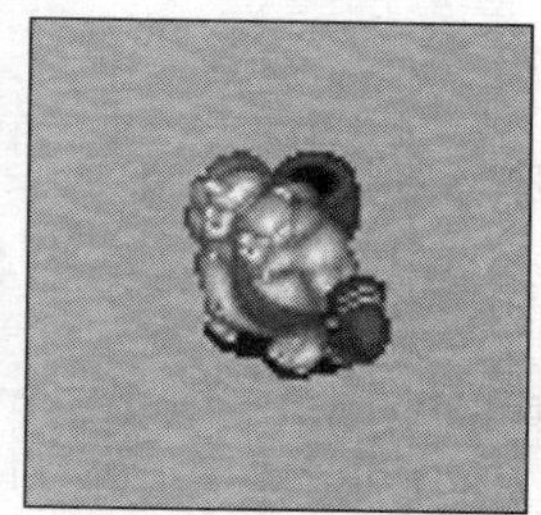

Visual Range:	5
Hit Points:	90
Magic Points:	0
Build Time:	90
Gold:	800
Lumber:	100
Oil:	0
Attack Range:	1
Armor:	4
Basic Damage:	8
Piercing Damage:	4
Effective Damage:	2–12
Speed:	13

The Ogre-Magi were originally a small band of extremely loyal Ogre enforcers, transformed by Gul'dan into scheming and malicious sorcerers. By warping and twisting the Elf-magicks of the Runestone at Caer Darrow, Gul'dan was able to infuse the magical abilities of long-dead Warlocks into the bodies of these unsuspecting hosts. Formerly hulking simpletons, the transformed Ogre-Magi can direct their death magicks as easily as their lesser cousins would deliver a crushing blow to anyone foolish enough to stand in their path. The Ogre-Magi have also become extremely cunning and insidious, serving the Horde only as they see fit.

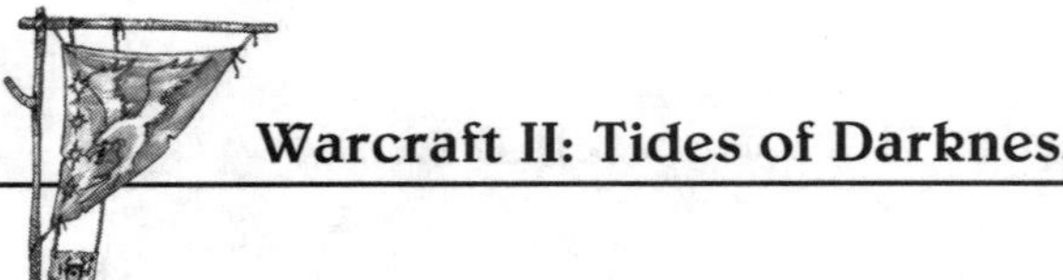

Ogre-Mage Spells

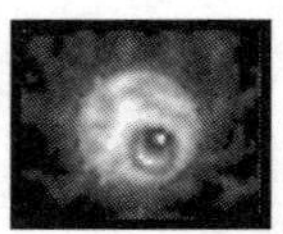

Eye of Kilrogg

Spell Point Cost: 70

The Ogre-Mage creates a free-floating apparition in the form of a disembodied Eye that he can then direct through the air to look down on enemy forces and encampments. Named for the great leader of the Bleeding Hollow clan, the ever-vigilant Eye transmits its view to the caster, giving him knowledge of the lands beneath it and those creatures who live in them. The Eye will vanish after a time, but the Ogre-Mage will retain his knowledge of the terrain.

Bloodlust

Spell Point Cost: 50

This enchantment is used to instill an insatiable lust for blood into a fellow warrior, causing him to enter into a savage, berserk rage. A fighter affected by Bloodlust does his opponents more damage than would normally be possible. Although this spell bestows no permanent effects on one enchanted by it, it has been known to push an already bloodthirsty Orc over the edge.

Runes

Spell Point Cost: 200

The casting of ancient and powerful Runes enables the Ogre-Mage to lay a subtle trap for those hapless enough to enter into it. When these Runes explode, they cause massive damage to anyone standing over them, as well as to all those in adjacent areas. The diligent and watchful will catch a

glimpse of the Rune as they approach it. The chaotic forces released by this enchantment cannot discern the difference between allies and enemies and will kill a friend as surely as a foe. Heed these warnings well because stepping on these Runes is hazardous—it will cause them to explode when their magicks are triggered.

Catapult

Visual Range:	9
Hit Points:	110
Magic Points:	–
Build Time:	250
Gold:	900
Lumber:	300
Oil:	–
Attack Range:	8
Armor:	0
Basic Damage:	80
Piercing Damage:	0
Effective Damage:	25–80
Speed:	5

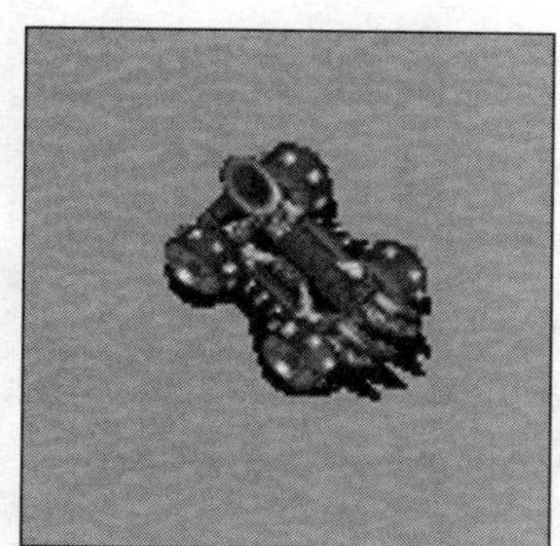

Sharpened horns, crimson with the blood of those unfortunate enough to be caught in their path, mark the appearance of the Orcish Catapult. Approaching on the battlefield, its grim exterior is enough to make the weak Human troops flee in stark terror. These cumbersome, wheeled machines launch deadly incendiary shot that explodes on impact. The sheer destructive force of these great engines of war makes them feared and respected throughout the land.

Death Knight

Visual Range:	9
Hit Points:	60
Magic Points:	255
Build Time:	120
Gold:	1,200
Lumber:	–
Oil:	–
Attack Range:	3
Armor:	0
Basic Damage:	–
Piercing Damage:	9
Effective Damage:	5–9
Speed:	8

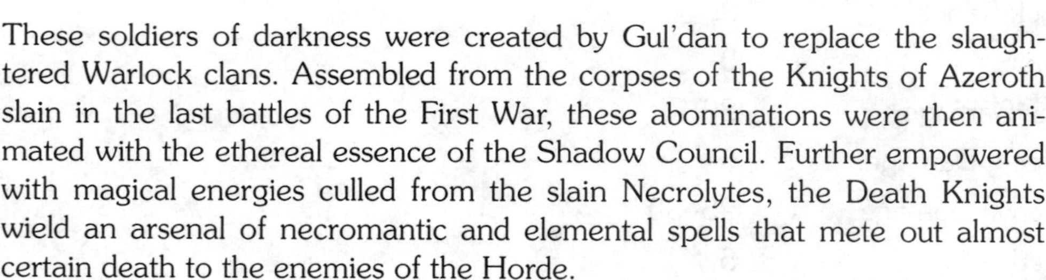

These soldiers of darkness were created by Gul'dan to replace the slaughtered Warlock clans. Assembled from the corpses of the Knights of Azeroth slain in the last battles of the First War, these abominations were then animated with the ethereal essence of the Shadow Council. Further empowered with magical energies culled from the slain Necrolytes, the Death Knights wield an arsenal of necromantic and elemental spells that mete out almost certain death to the enemies of the Horde.

Death Knight Spells

Touch of Darkness

By enveloping their truncheons with the dark essence of Hades, the Death Knights are able to rob foes of their vital energy. The ability of the Death Knights to discharge this energy over short distances makes them particularly menacing. Although the effects of this spell are abhorrent to the living, the

Touch of Darkness is but a lesser enchantment within the arsenal of these vile horsemen.

Death Coil

Spell Point Cost: 100

Death Coil is a particularly potent variation of the Touch of Darkness spell. By channeling the necromantic powers of the underworld through his ghoulish form, the Death Knight creates a field of dark energy that drains the life force from any who come in contact with it. This life force is then consumed—thereby replenishing the strength of the caster. The icy embrace of death can be beneficial . . . for those who know how to control it.

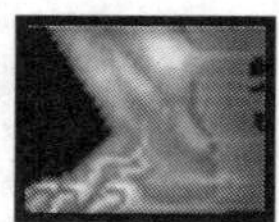

Haste

Spell Point Cost: 50

By magically increasing the speed at which a body generates vital energy, the caster may bestow great speed on any being. All actions taken by one so enchanted are swifter than those of a common adversary—an obvious advantage on the battlefield. The effects of Haste persist for only a short time.

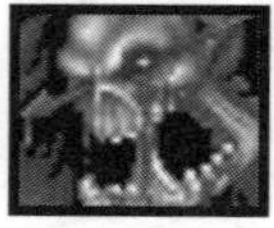

Raise Dead

Spell Point Cost: 50 per Skeleton

This dark magic is the final legacy of the Orc Necrolytes who were destroyed shortly after the First War. Death Knights can animate the newly dead and then command these monstrosities to attack their enemies. This terrifying spell constitutes the paramount power of the Death Knights, because it serves to augment the Horde forces with vast armies of the undead.

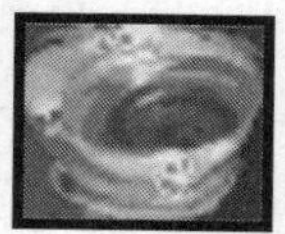

Whirlwind

Spell Point Cost: 100

This focusing of the winds of the underworld causes any caught within it to be cast about with violent force. Bones are easily shattered and mainsails quickly snapped by these fierce winds. The winds' howl allow no commands to be issued to those trapped within the Whirlwind, rendering those unfortunates helpless until the magicks fade.

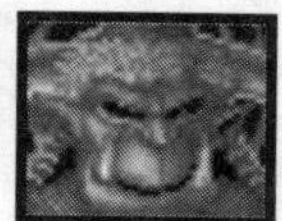

Unholy Armor

Spell Point Cost: 100

This ancient Necromantic spell transforms a portion of the recipient's life force into an unearthly, phantasmal suit of armor. This spectral armor then absorbs the damage from any attack directed at its wearer for a limited period of time. As the magicks that link this armor to its host vanish, so will the wearer's invulnerability.

Death and Decay

Spell Point Cost: 25 per barrage

The dark, swirling clouds conjured by the Death Knights can cause anything within their path to rot and decompose. The vapor created by Decay can consume anything—flesh, bone, wood, or even the strongest metal. Heavily laden with base substances, these clouds descend and quickly diffuse, leaving only suffering in their wake.

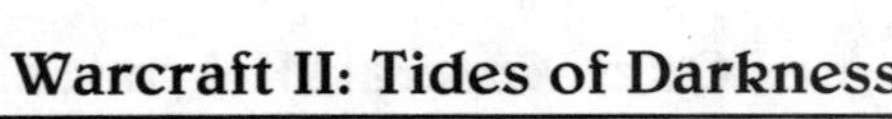

Goblin Sapper

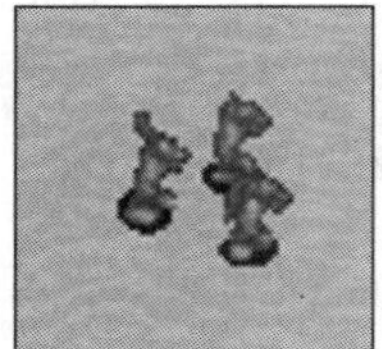

Visual Range:	4
Hit Points:	40
Magic Points:	0
Build Time:	200
Gold:	700
Lumber:	250
Oil:	0
Attack Range:	1
Armor:	0
Basic Damage:	4
Piercing Damage:	2
Effective Damage:	1–6
Explosive Damage:	400
Speed:	11

The mischievous Goblin Sappers are known throughout the Horde for their tremendous aptitude for destruction. These diabolical Goblins are invariably armed with extremely volatile explosives; these enable them to level enemy structures and weapon emplacements. Although the Sappers are highly unpredictable and insubordinate, they have become necessary to the Horde's plans of conquest.

Zeppelin

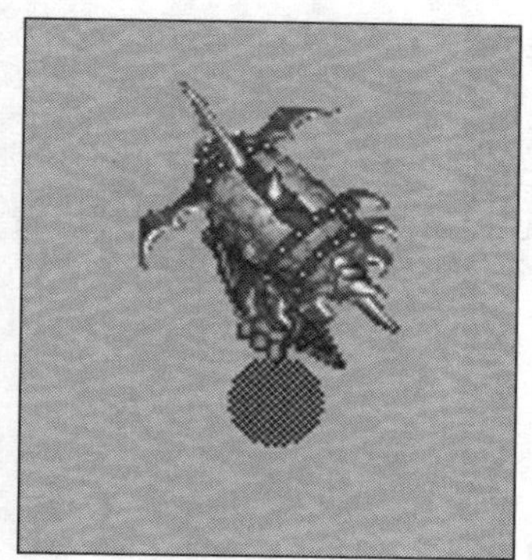

Visual Range:	9
Hit Points:	150
Magic Points:	–
Build Time:	65
Gold:	500
Lumber:	100
Oil:	–
Attack Range:	–
Armor:	2
Basic Damage:	–
Piercing Damage:	–
Effective Damage:	–
Speed:	17

Zeppelins are ingenious inventions that allow small teams of Goblins to soar above the countryside and spy on enemy positions. The Zeppelins are cumbersome and awkward, and maintain no armament. Their airborne capabilities and their extensive line of sight, however, make them an integral part of the Horde's spy network.

Dragon

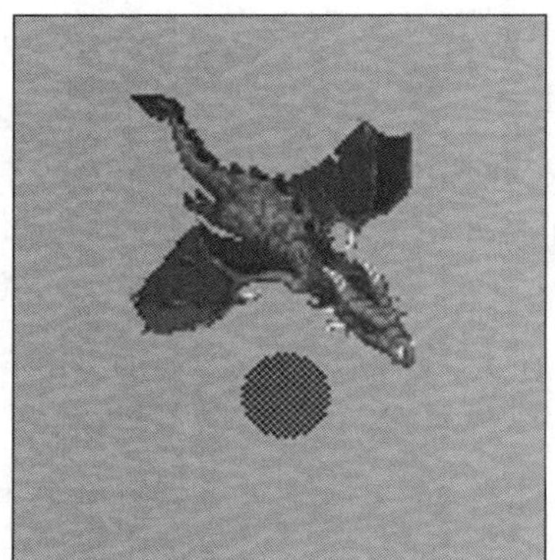

Visual Range:	6
Hit Points:	100
Magic Points:	–
Build Time:	250
Gold:	2,500
Lumber:	–
Oil:	–
Attack Range:	4
Armor:	5
Basic Damage:	0
Piercing Damage:	16
Effective Damage:	8–16
Speed:	14

Dragons are native to the untamed northlands of Azeroth. Reclusive by nature, Dragons have had little contact with their earthbound neighbors over the centuries. Rend and Maim, the Chieftains of the Black Tooth Grin clan, masterminded the capture of the Dragon Queen, Alexstrasza. With their Queen held captive, these majestic creatures have been forced into subservience by the Horde; her progeny are raised by the Dragonmaw clan to slaughter the enemies of the Horde.

With their tremendous destructive powers and keen intellects, the Dragons represent the single most powerful force within the Horde. The devastating flame that issues from the mouths of older serpents can level any number of enemy troops; their powerful wings allow them to soar tirelessly through the skies.

Oil Tanker

Visual Range:	4
Hit Points:	90
Magic Points:	–
Build Time:	50
Gold:	400
Lumber:	200
Oil:	–
Attack Range:	–
Armor:	10
Basic Damage:	–
Piercing Damage:	–
Effective Damage:	–
Speed:	10

The Orcish Oil Tanker is crudely constructed because its purpose is for bearing cargo rather than weapons or troops. The Tanker, consisting of little more than a collection of wood, bone, and storage space, is crewed by a mob of Orcs scarcely more capable than the lowly Peons. Other than being able to pilot the craft, the crew of the Tanker performs tasks equivalent to those of a Peon—building Oil Platforms and returning cargo to be processed and used as the overseer directs.

Troll Destroyer

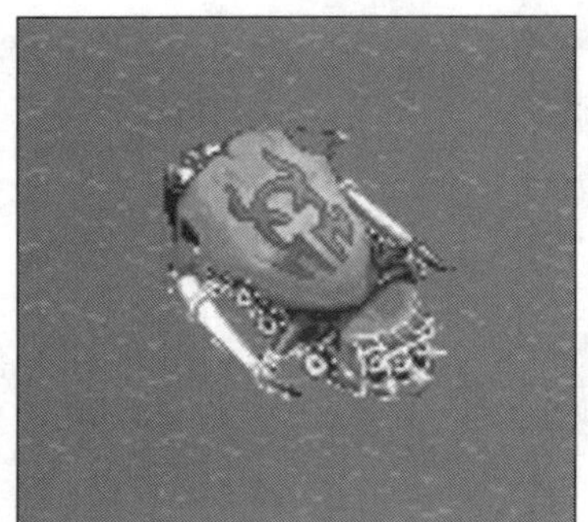

Visual Range:	8
Hit Points:	100
Magic Points:	–
Build Time:	90
Gold:	700
Lumber:	350
Oil:	700
Attack Range:	4
Armor:	10
Basic Damage:	35
Piercing Damage:	0
Effective Damage:	2–35
Speed:	10

The Troll Destroyers are swift, ill-formed longboats designed to cut through enemy armadas and deal damage to enemy vessels. The savage Troll crewmen are eager to enter into combat against Alliance ships of war and hungrily await any chance to stand mast-to-mast against the Elven Destroyers.

TRANSPORT

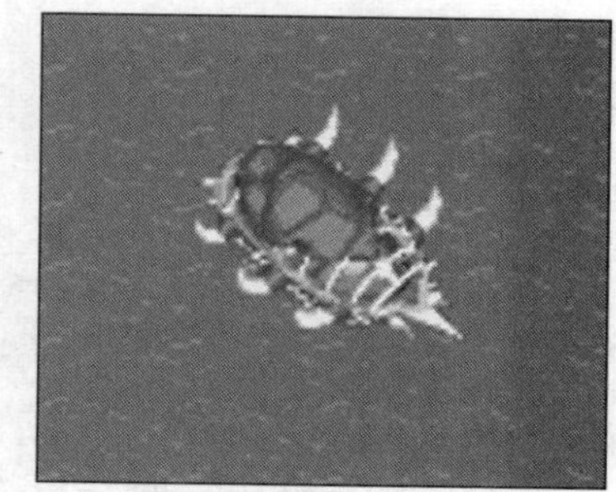

Visual Range:	4
Hit Points:	150
Magic Points:	–
Build Time:	70
Gold:	600
Lumber:	200
Oil:	500
Attack Range:	–
Armor:	0
Basic Damage:	–
Piercing Damage:	–
Effective Damage:	–
Speed:	10

Transports are huge skeletal ships charged with ferrying Horde troops across large bodies of water. Being slow and bulky, Transports rely upon magical armor to repel enemy fire. Although the Horde is known to defend its Transports with Destroyers and Juggernaughts, some reckless crews will sail straight into a naval engagement to deliver their troops to land.

Ogre Juggernaught

Visual Range:	8
Hit Points:	150
Magic Points:	–
Build Time:	140
Gold:	1,000
Lumber:	500
Oil:	1,000
Attack Range:	6
Armor:	15
Basic Damage:	130
Piercing Damage:	0
Effective Damage:	50–130
Speed:	6

These gargantuan ships of war are the main armament in the dark armada of the Horde. Heavily armed and armored, the Juggernaughts are veritable floating fortresses; they are the greatest implements of destruction within the Horde's naval forces. Though not as swift as the Troll warships, these ruinous craft have quickly come to be feared across the seas of Azeroth for their unrelenting onslaughts against the Alliance.

Giant Turtle

Visual Range:	5
Hit Points:	60
Magic Points:	–
Build Time:	100
Gold:	800
Lumber:	150
Oil:	900
Attack Range:	4
Armor:	0
Basic Damage:	50
Piercing Damage:	0
Effective Damage:	10–50
Speed:	7

These giant sea turtles are native to the southern seas; they were captured by the Stormreaver clan. Pacified by potent spells of control, these lumbering monstrosities are fitted with watertight canopies strapped onto the backs of their shells and are used as submersible Orcish craft. By submerging themselves under the waves, the Giant Turtles can steal up on unsuspecting enemy craft and report their positions to the Horde fleet. The daring Goblins who control them are dedicated to destroying enemy ships by any means necessary.

METZEN
·95·

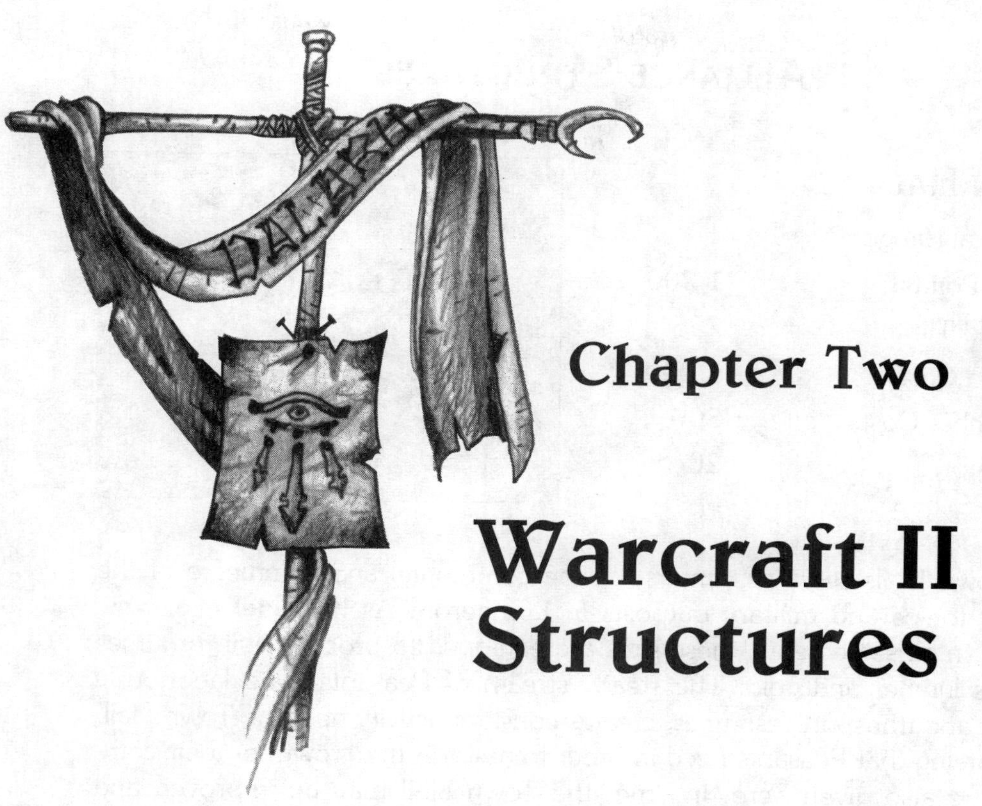

Chapter Two

Warcraft II Structures

"Do you know what horrors lie beyond those walls?"

—Valeria, *Conan the Barbarian*

Medieval armies do not have the luxury of having everything shipped in for a battle. Artisans and workers must set up villages near the battle site to provide housing, food, and weapons in preparation for war. This chapter details everything you need to know about building your own Rome in a day.

Alliance Structures

Town Hall

Visual Range:	4
Hit Points:	1,200
Build Time:	255
Gold Cost:	1,200
Lumber Cost:	800
Armor:	20

The Town Halls serve as centers for the community and commerce of the various towns and military outposts in Lordaeron. As the chief economic centers in all settlements, these sites are equipped to process vital resources such as lumber and gold. The steady stream of Peasants, who laboriously harvest and transport resources, creates constant activity near the Town Hall. The training that Peasants need in order to assist in the growth of their community is also given here. In time, the Town Hall may be improved and upgraded into a Keep.

Options:

Train Peasant

Upgrade to Keep

Requires Barracks

KEEP

Visual Range:	6
Hit Points:	1,400
Build Time:	200
Gold Cost:	2,000
Lumber Cost:	1,000
Oil Cost:	200
Armor:	20
Production:	Gold 100+10

In large and well-defended settlements, the Keep replaces the Town Hall as the center of commerce where Peasants can deliver shipments of gold and lumber for processing. The Keep is also a military structure protected by high granite walls, which make it difficult to destroy. Advancing legions of Orcish warriors force the Alliance to assign its elite troops—the Knights of Lordaeron and the mysterious Elven Rangers—only to such places where their presence will serve to deny the Horde further strategic gains. As control of these towns becomes more critical, the Keep may need to be upgraded into a Castle.

OPTIONS:

Train Peasant

Upgrade to Castle

Requires Stables, Blacksmith, Lumber Mill

CASTLE

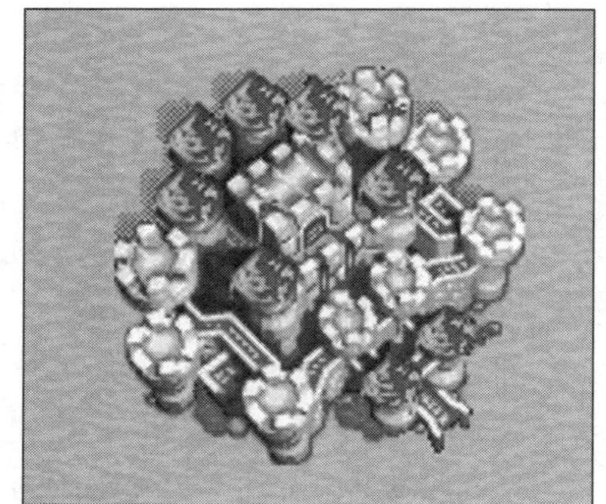

Visual Range:	9
Hit Points:	1,600
Build Time:	200
Gold Cost:	2,500
Lumber Cost:	1,200
Oil Cost:	500
Armor:	20
Production:	Gold 100+20

The mighty Castles of Lordaeron are the centers of large military cities. As in the lesser Keeps, Peasants may bring gold and lumber here for judicious distribution in order to sustain the war effort. These bastions against invasion are guarded by fortified battlements, which make them virtually indestructible. The Castle represents the strength of the peoples of the Alliance and their unyielding resolution to defend the whole of humanity against the Orcish Hordes.

OPTIONS:

Train Peasant

Farm

Visual Range:	3
Hit Points:	400
Build Time:	100
Gold Cost:	500
Lumber Cost:	250
Armor:	20

Farms are a vital part of the many communities in Lordaeron. Producing various grains and foodstuffs, Farms generate sustenance not only for peasants and workers, but for armies as well. The overall amount of food produced by a town's Farms is a major factor in determining the number of new workers or soldiers that the community can accommodate. It is imperative that this production be monitored at all times, so that the population remains well fed and the town runs smoothly.

Barracks

Visual Range:	3
Hit Points:	800
Build Time:	200
Gold Cost:	700
Lumber Cost:	450
Armor:	20

Barracks are large fortified structures that offer training and housing for the many warriors of the Alliance. An integral part of any defended community, the Barracks foster unity and good will between the races. Human Footmen live alongside Elven Archers; all train together under one roof. The training of Ballista crews and the construction of these war machines also take place within the Barracks compound.

Options:

Train Footman

Train Archer

Requires Lumber Mill

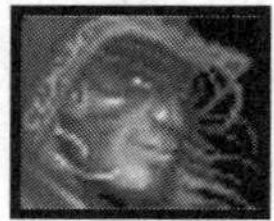

Train Ranger

Requires Keep, Lumber Mill, Ranger Upgrade

Replaces Archer

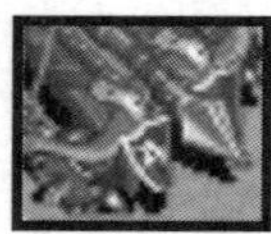

Train Ballista

Requires Lumber Mill, Blacksmith

Train Knight

Requires Stables

Train Paladin

Requires Stables, Church, Paladin Upgrade

Replaces Knight

Elven Lumber Mill

Visual Range:	3
Hit Points:	600
Build Time:	150
Gold Cost:	600
Lumber Cost:	450
Armor:	20
Production:	Lumber 100+25

Seeking insight into the mysteries of the great Ironwood trees of Northeron, the Elves of Quel'thalas constructed Lumber Mills and became exceptional craftsmen. The Elves offered their superior skills to the Alliance, providing more efficient means for processing lumber. The production of ships and war machines becomes possible with the addition of these structures.

Lumber Mills are also responsible for producing the perfectly crafted arrows that make the Elven Archers feared throughout the Horde. When given the necessary resources, Elven craftsmen will upgrade the quality of these arrows, increasing the possible damage that can be inflicted by them. Elven Rangers, after being trained at the Barracks, have been known to gather at the mills, honing the skills of Longbow, Marksmanship, and Scouting.

Options:

Upgrade Arrows 1

Damage +1

Build Time: 200

Gold: 300

Lumber: 300

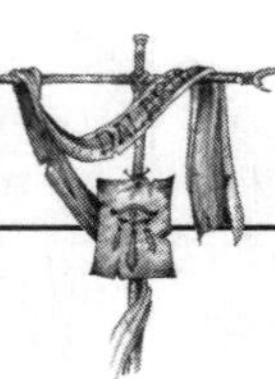

Upgrade Arrows 2

Damage +1

Build Time: 250

Gold: 900

Lumber: 500

Elven Ranger Training

Requires Keep

Build Time: 250

Gold: 1,500

Scouting Research

Sight 9

Build Time: 250

Gold: 1,500

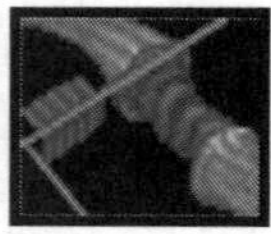

Longbow Research

Range +1

Build Time: 250

Gold: 2,000

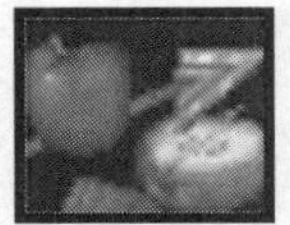

Marksmanship Research

Damage +3

Build Time: 250

Gold: 2,500

BLACKSMITH

Visual Range:	3
Hit Points:	775
Build Time:	200
Gold Cost:	800
Lumber Cost:	450
Oil Cost:	100
Armor:	20

Blacksmiths are important to many settlements that are dependent on military protection. Although the metals forged by Blacksmiths are vital to the construction of advanced buildings, Blacksmiths are especially known for their skills of weapon crafting and armoring. The smiths of Lordaeron, occasionally aided by their skillful Dwarven allies, are renowned for producing some of the finest-quality weapons in the northlands. The Blacksmiths and Elves are rumored to be developing a machine that may alter the course of the war against the Horde.

OPTIONS:

Upgrade Swords 1

Damage +2

Build Time: 200

Gold: 800

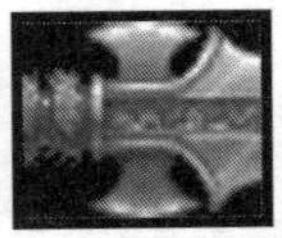

Upgrade Swords 2

Damage +2

Build Time: 250

Gold: 2,400

Upgrade Shields 1

Armor +2

Build Time: 200

Gold: 300

Lumber: 300

Upgrade Shields 2

Armor +2

Build Time: 250

Gold: 900

Lumber: 500

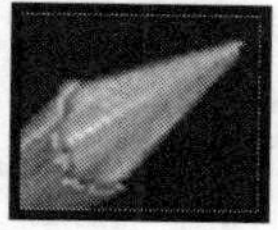

Upgrade Ballista 1

Damage +15

Build Time: 250

Gold: 1,500

Upgrade Ballista 2

Damage +15

Build Time: 250

Gold: 4,000

Scout Tower

Visual Range:	9
Hit Points:	100
Build Time:	60
Gold Cost:	550
Lumber Cost:	200
Armor:	20

Scout Towers are tall, sturdy structures constructed to guard the borders of many settlements. From these sites, the defenders of Lordaeron can spot enemy troops from high above, making it difficult for the Orcs to launch surprise attacks. The presence of these structures in the wildlands ensures the swift deployment of our armies to meet any Orc incursion.

Options:

Upgrade to Guard Tower

Requires Lumber Mill

Upgrade to Cannon Tower

Requires Blacksmith

Guard Tower

Visual Range:	9
Attack Range:	6
Hit Points:	130
Build Time:	140
Gold Cost:	500
Lumber Cost:	150
Armor:	20
Basic Damage:	4
Piercing Damage:	12
Effective Damage:	6–16

Once upgraded, the Guard Tower houses a small Ballista for limited stationary defense. Such a structure cannot be upgraded again into a Cannon Tower.

Cannon Tower

Visual Range:	9
Attack Range:	7
Hit Points:	160
Build Time:	190
Gold Cost:	1,000
Lumber Cost:	300
Armor:	20
Basic Damage:	50
Piercing Damage:	0
Effective Damage:	10–50

Although twice as expensive as the Guard Tower, Cannon Towers provide a formidable stationary defense and a slightly longer firing range. A row of these along a shoreline can pelt enemy ships and sink them long before they even threaten to attack.

Stables

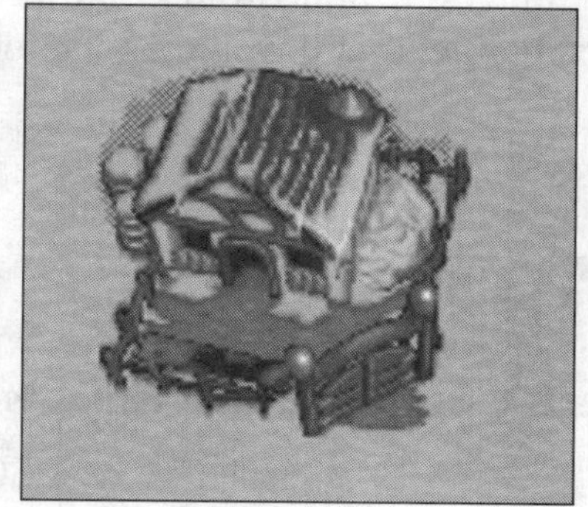

Visual Range:	3
Hit Points:	500
Build Time:	150
Gold Cost:	1,000
Lumber Cost:	300
Armor:	20

Stables are maintained to breed and house Lordaeron's prized warhorses. Determined to condition the horses to be faster, stronger, and more responsive to their riders, the trainers at these sites take great pride in their work.

These brave and loyal stallions carry Knights into battle and also contribute precious fertilizer to the bountiful farms about Lordaeron. The Stables are manned by dependable horsemen and stablehands who tend to the steeds with great devotion.

Church

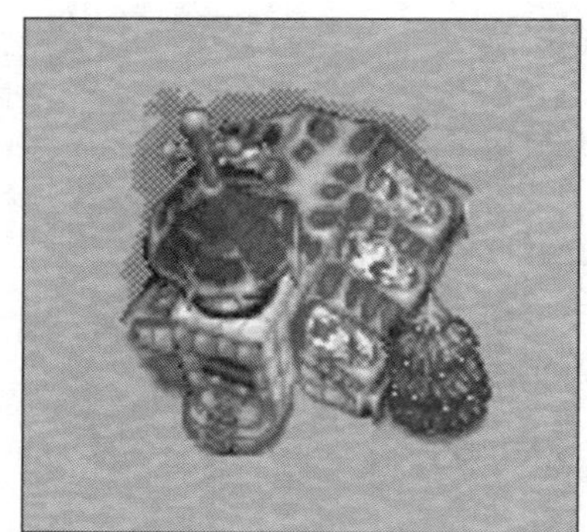

Visual Range:	3
Hit Points:	700
Build Time:	175
Gold Cost:	900
Lumber Cost:	500
Armor:	20

Churches are places where the citizens of Lordaeron seek spiritual enlightenment. Once led by devout Clerics, Churches now depend on Paladins to minister to the masses in this time of war. It is in these places of healing and serenity that the holy warriors gather to deepen their faith. Through meditating, communing, and tithing at these sacred sites, Paladins discover new ways to channel their healing and spiritual powers.

Options:

Upgrade Knights to Paladins

Build Time: 250

Gold: 1,000

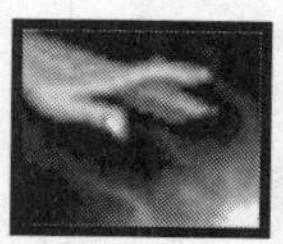

Research Healing

Build Time: 200

Gold: 1,000

Research Exorcism

Build Time: 200

Gold: 2,000

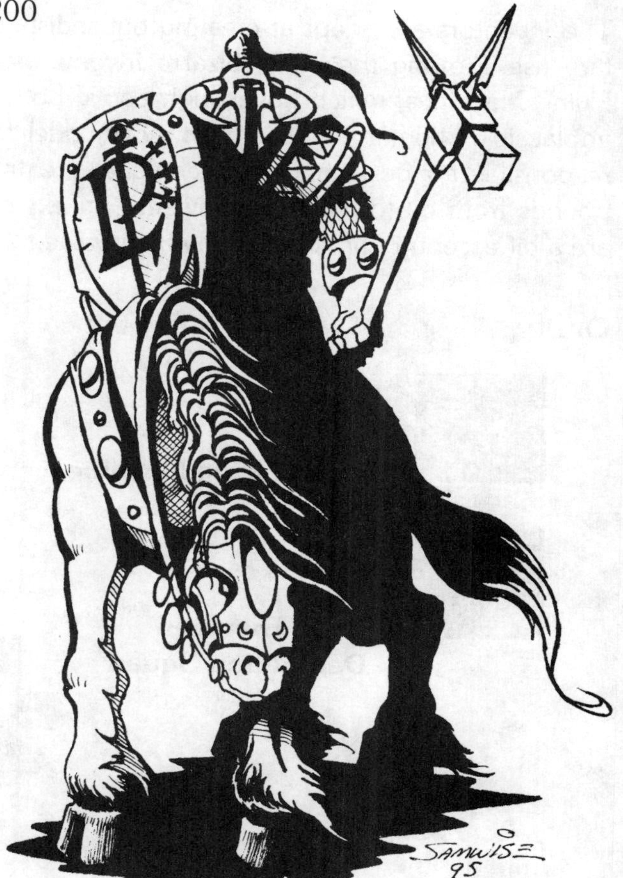

Gnomish Inventor

Visual Range:	3
Hit Points:	500
Build Time:	150
Gold Cost:	1,000
Lumber Cost:	400
Armor:	20

The Inventors are adept at creating outlandishly clever contraptions for military use. Among the many bizarre inventions created by the Gnomes are Flying Machines, which hover high above both land and sea, as well as the implausible Submarine, which can move under the sea. The Gnomes are also responsible for perfecting the technique of extracting various chemical compounds from oil to make gunpowder and explosives. Although the Gnomes are a bit eccentric, none can deny their value to the Alliance.

Options:

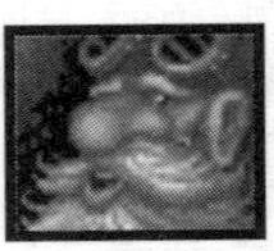

Build Flying Machine

Train Dwarven Demolition Squad

Mage Tower

Visual Range:	3
Hit Points:	500
Build Time:	125
Gold Cost:	1,000
Lumber Cost:	200
Armor:	20

Serpentine spires of living rock form the foundation of the Mage Towers, where glowing spheres of mystic energy replenish and focus the awesome magicks wielded against the Orcish Horde. These Towers hold ominous secrets that none but the Mages of Lordaeron dare explore. As extensions of the Violet Citadel in Dalaran, these Towers allow the Mages to research arcane spells, unhindered by the affairs of the temporal plane.

Options:

Train Mage

Research Slow

Build Time: 100

Gold: 500

Research Flame Shield

Build Time: 100

Gold: 1,000

Research Invisibility

Build Time: 200

Gold: 2,500

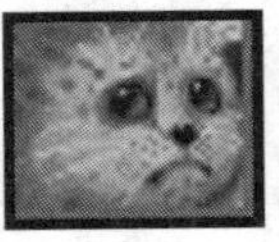

Research Polymorph

Build Time: 200

Gold: 2,000

Research Blizzard

Build Time: 200

Gold: 2,000

Gryphon Aviary

Visual Range:	3
Hit Points:	500
Build Time:	150
Gold Cost:	1,000
Lumber Cost:	400
Armor:	20

Constructed in homage to the legendary beasts housed within, the colossal structure of the Gryphon Aviary looms over all that it surveys. Hewn from solid rock by the Dwarves of Northeron, their Aviary inspires dread in the

heart of anyone considered a foe by these Gryphon Riders. Deep inside this massive edifice are the Gryphon aeries, as well as the Dwarven workshops where saddles and harnesses are crafted.

Most sacred to the Dwarves is the enchanted forge that lies at the heart of each Aviary. It is here that the magical weapons known as Stormhammers are fashioned. A Stormhammer, when thrown, strikes with the fury of lightning and the force of thunder. This destructive weapon, combined with the indomitable spirit of the Gryphon Riders, justifies their reputation as masters of the skies.

Options:

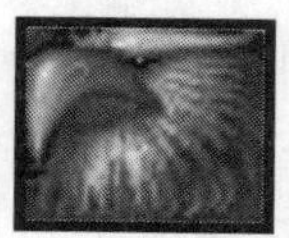

Train Gryphon Rider

Shipyard

Visual Range:	3
Hit Points:	1,100
Build Time:	200
Gold Cost:	800
Lumber Cost:	450
Armor:	20

Shipyards are primarily responsible for the construction of the various warships in the Alliance's naval forces. Elevated on strong pillars of Ironwood, these waterfront structures are also responsible for receiving and processing the oil necessary to construct ships of war. Shipyards are manned by dedicated sailors and shipwrights, who strive tirelessly to keep the fleet running smoothly.

Options:

Build Oil Tanker

Build Destroyer

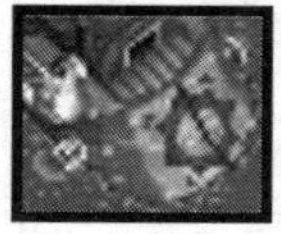

Build Transport

Requires Foundry

Build Battleship

Requires Foundry

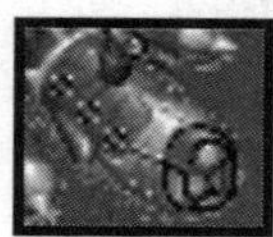

Build Gnomish Submarine

Requires Gnomish Inventor

Foundry

Visual Range:	3
Hit Points:	750
Build Time:	175
Gold Cost:	700
Lumber Cost:	400
Oil Cost:	400
Armor:	20

The introduction of Foundries makes possible the construction of the mighty vessels known as Transports and Battleships. Obsessed with creating the strongest force in the Alliance, the skilled Foundry artisans need only ample resources to design better armor and weaponry for the fleet. Located on the coast to easier supplement Alliance Shipyards, they are an integral part of warship maintenance. Constantly filled with heavy clouds of soot and ash, the intense heat that radiates from the huge smelting pools inspires some to jest that they may be in an Orcish building instead of a Human one.

Options:

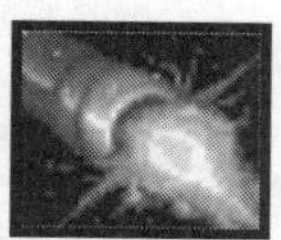

Upgrade Ship Cannons 1

Damage +5

Build Time: 200

Gold: 700

Lumber: 100

Oil: 1,000

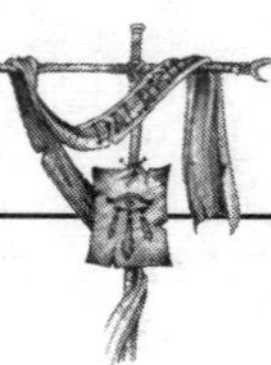

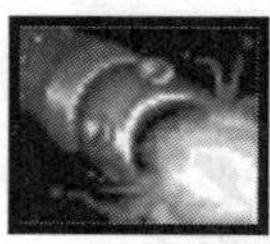

Upgrade Ship Cannons 2

Damage +5

Build Time: 250

Gold: 2,000

Lumber: 250

Oil: 3,000

Upgrade Ship Armor 1

Armor +5

Build Time: 200

Gold: 500

Lumber: 500

Upgrade Ship Armor 2

Armor +5

Build Time: 250

Gold: 1,500

Lumber: 900

Oil Refinery

Visual Range:	3
Hit Points:	600
Build Time:	225
Gold Cost:	800
Lumber Cost:	350
Oil Cost:	200
Armor:	20
Production:	Oil 100+25

These large steel-clad buildings are designed for the refining of raw oil to be used in the construction and maintenance of the Alliance fleets, as well as for the creation of unconventional war machines. Like a Shipyard, a Refinery is built on the coast so that Tankers can deliver their cargo directly to its doors. A Refinery allows oil to be processed with far greater efficiency than a Shipyard alone.

Oil Platform

Visual Range:	3
Hit Points:	650
Build Time:	200
Gold Cost:	700
Lumber Cost:	450
Armor:	20

The vast amounts of oil beneath the sea must be used for the construction of ships and various war machines. Because the oceans are rich with this substance, Tankers need to construct platforms in areas where the oil is thick. Only then can the Tankers collect their dark cargo. As the Horde drew near Lordaeron and the seas became increasingly treacherous, the Platforms that had been built by Human drillers before the Great War were destroyed.

Horde Structures

Great Hall

Visual Range:	4
Hit Points:	1,200
Build Time:	255
Gold Cost:	1,200
Lumber Cost:	800
Armor:	20

This structure serves many purposes. It is the gathering place and command center for most Orcish settlements. The lowly Peons, who are unfit for battle, are trained here to perform the menial tasks of construction, repair, and harvesting. This is also where vital raw materials are gathered to be processed and then distributed. The Great Hall is always a source of feverish activity as the Peons labor to please their overseers. When a settlement achieves greater prosperity and requires stronger defenses, the Great Hall can be reinforced to make it a Stronghold.

Options:

Train Peon

Upgrade to Stronghold

Requires Barracks

STRONGHOLD

Visual Range:	6
Hit Points:	1,400
Build Time:	200
Gold Cost:	2,000
Lumber Cost:	1,000
Oil Cost:	200
Armor:	20
Production:	Gold 100+10

The massive, jagged spires of the Orc Stronghold are a constant reminder to the Horde of Orcish power and dominance. As the center of a large Orcish settlement, the Stronghold can process gold and lumber in the same fashion as a Great Hall. Techniques are used in the construction of these intimidating steel and stone structures to make them capable of serving as strong barriers, greatly reducing the damage inflicted by attacking forces. Convinced of their innate superiority as warriors, Ogres and Troll Berserkers will act only under the direction of an overseer who has proven himself capable enough to establish a Stronghold. As need and resources dictate, a Stronghold can be reinforced and refitted as a Fortress.

OPTIONS:

Train Peon

Upgrade to Fortress

Requires Ogre Mound, Blacksmith, Lumber Mill

FORTRESS

Visual Range:	9
Hit Points:	1,600
Build Time:	200
Gold Cost:	2,500
Lumber Cost:	1,200
Oil Cost:	500
Armor:	20
Production:	Gold 100+20

As the military and economic center of each of the largest Orc cities, the Fortress can hold and process all the gold and lumber that the Peons can be made to harvest. Protected by obsidian spires, the Fortress is all but impervious to the attacks of the feeble Human forces. Constructed by Orcish leaders who have attained the greatest mastery both on and off the field of battle, the Fortress serves as a proclamation to the Alliance of the inevitable triumph of the Orcish Horde.

OPTIONS:

Train Peon

Pig Farm

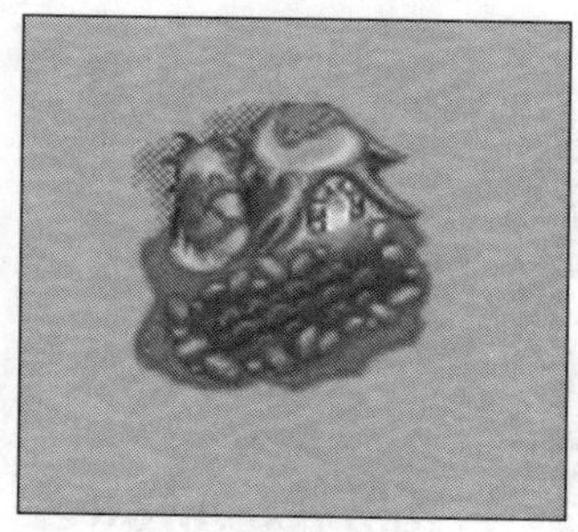

Visual Range:	3
Hit Points:	400
Build Time:	100
Gold Cost:	500
Lumber Cost:	250
Armor:	20

Farms provide the raw foodstuffs necessary to sustain both the slave labor force and the war parties in the field. Without a sufficient food supply, new units cannot be acquired. The staple diet of the Orcs—like that of their Troll and Ogre kin—is fresh meat. To satisfy this hunger for flesh, wild Boars are trapped and bred for food. Abundant in most regions, they have become a bonfire favorite (along with a tankard of Bloodmead) for hardened troops engaged in a long war march.

Barracks

Visual Range:	3
Hit Points:	800
Build Time:	200
Gold Cost:	700
Lumber Cost:	450
Armor:	20

The most highly honored structure in any Orcish community, the Barracks maintains the necessary facilities to train Orc, Troll, and Ogre troops for battle. The clash of cold steel and the war cries of Troll Axethrowers can be heard from dawn until dusk, providing a constant reminder of the warlike mentality of the Horde.

OPTIONS:

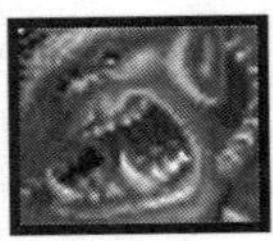

Train Grunt

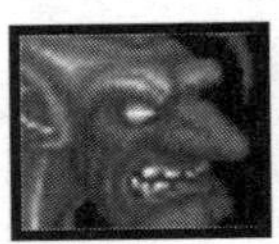

Train Axethrower

Requires Lumber Mill

Build Catapult

Requires Blacksmith

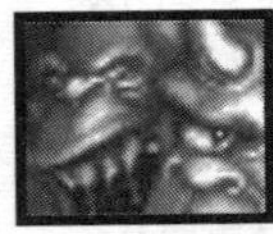

Build Two-Headed Ogre

Requires Ogre Mound

Train Berserker

Requires Stronghold, Lumber Mill, Berserker Upgrade

Train Ogre-Mage

Requires Ogre Mound, Altar of Storms, Ogre-Mage Upgrade

Troll Lumber Mill

Visual Range:	3
Hit Points:	600
Build Time:	150
Gold Cost:	600
Lumber Cost:	450
Armor:	20
Production:	Lumber 100+25

Carved from the husk of an ancient Ironwood tree, the Troll Lumber Mill is a vital part of the Horde's lumber-processing operation. The Trolls, having lived in the forests of the far north for centuries, have devised a unique method of harvesting. By treating a group of trees with a volatile alchemical solvent, the Trolls can deaden and weaken large sections of wood.

Trolls have become quite adept at fashioning a special sort of throwing axe. The making and the use of this weapon are always being perfected. Troll Berserkers frequent the Ironwood trees to digest potions given to them by the Goblin Alchemists stationed in their environs. These potions sharpen the sight of the Berserkers or give them the ability to throw their axes over greater distances. It is said that the speed at which healing occurs can be increased by ingesting the correct potion. This process of regeneration, or fast healing, is one of the most unusual and awesome powers of the Troll Berserkers.

Options:

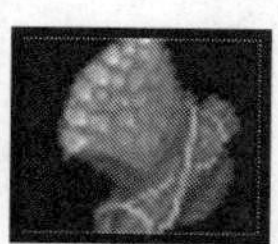

Upgrade Throwing Axes 1

Damage +1

Build Time: 200

Gold: 300

Lumber: 300

Upgrade Throwing Axes 2

Damage +1

Build Time: 250

Gold: 900

Lumber: 500

Berserker Upgrade

Requires Stronghold

Build Time: 250

Gold: 1,500

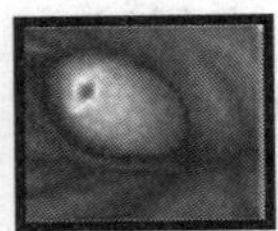

Berserker Scouting

Sight: 9

Build Time: 250

Gold: 1,500

Research Lighter Axes

Range +1

Build Time: 250

Gold: 2,000

Berserker Regeneration

Build Time: 250

Gold: 3,000

Blacksmith

Visual Range:	3
Hit Points:	775
Build Time:	200
Gold Cost:	800
Lumber Cost:	450
Oil Cost:	100
Armor:	20

The Orcs that live and work in the Blacksmith shops are veteran warriors themselves. Understanding the value of strong steel, they are always developing new techniques to improve their weapons or upgrade the quality of their armor. The steel that they forge is essential to manufacture the devastating Catapult. Their expertise is also often required for the construction of advanced structures.

Options:

Upgrade Weapons 1

Damage +2

Build Time: 200

Gold: 500

Lumber: 100

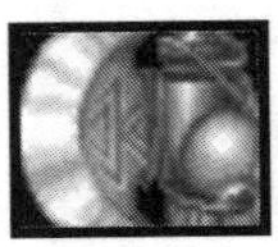

Upgrade Weapons 2

Damage +2

Build Time: 250

Gold: 1,500

Lumber: 300

Upgrade Shields 1

Armor +2

Build Time: 200

Gold: 300

Lumber: 300

Upgrade Shields 2

Armor +2

Build Time: 250

Gold: 900

Lumber: 500

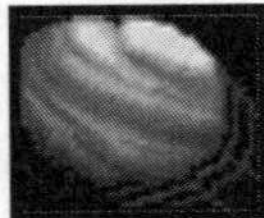

Upgrade Catapults 1

Damage +15

Build Time: 250

Gold: 1,500

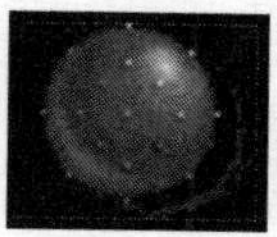

Upgrade Catapults 2

Damage +15

Build Time: 250

Gold: 4,000

Scout Tower

Visual Range:	9
Hit Points:	100
Build Time:	60
Gold Cost:	550
Lumber Cost:	200
Armor:	20

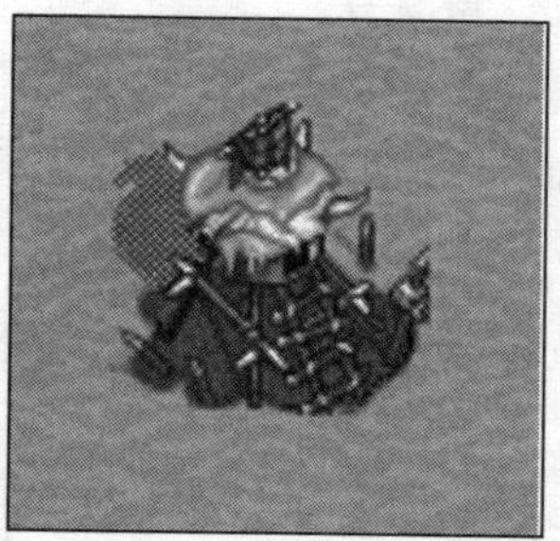

Rising high above the timberline, Scout Towers resemble primitive huts, decked with animal bones and giant tusks of every kind. These insubstantial, but highly useful, lookout posts are ideal for spotting the cowardly and deceitful Human forces from above; this makes them a useful part of any Orcish settlement's defenses.

Guard Tower

Visual Range:	9
Weapons Range:	6
Hit Points:	130
Build Time:	140
Gold Cost:	500
Lumber Cost:	150
Armor:	20
Basic Damage:	4
Piercing Damage:	12
Effective Damage:	6–16

Once upgraded, the Guard Tower houses a small Ballista for limited stationary defense. Such a structure cannot be upgraded again into a Cannon Tower.

Cannon Tower

Visual Range:	9
Weapons Range:	7
Hit Points:	160
Build Time:	190
Gold Cost:	1,000
Lumber Cost:	300
Armor:	20
Basic Damage:	50
Piercing Damage:	0
Effective Damage:	10–50

Although twice as expensive as Guard Towers, Cannon Towers provide a formidable stationary defense and a slightly longer firing range. A row of these along a shoreline can pelt enemy ships and sink them long before they become a threat.

Ogre Mound

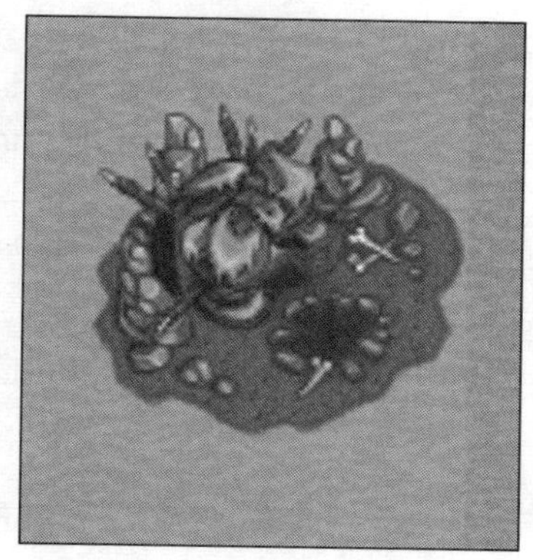

Visual Range:	3
Hit Points:	500
Build Time:	150
Gold Cost:	1,000
Lumber Cost:	300
Armor:	20

After being trained in the rudiments of combat at the Barracks, Ogres congregate in these crude stone huts to enhance their endurance, strength, and speed. These two-headed titans increase their great strength by engaging in contests that involve the hurling and crushing of giant rocks. This increases their already formidable strength and resilience; those that do escape the pounding delivered by their brethren find themselves the quicker for it. Even the half-wit Peons dare not come near this place, for stray boulders tend to descend on the heads of unwary visitors.

Altar of Storms

Visual Range:	3
Hit Points:	700
Build Time:	175
Gold Cost:	900
Lumber Cost:	500
Armor:	20

Carved from the Runestone at Caer Darrow, the Altar of Storms channels dark energies through the bronze figures that tower above it to pervert the innate Elven magicks of the Runestone. These energies, which were lost when the Orc Warlocks were destroyed by the Doomhammer, are now used to create the powers of the Ogre-Magi. It is here that the Ogre-Magi are

given new spells and skills to aid them in their fight against the Alliance. The Altars are avoided by the rest of the Horde because the intense energies that emanate from their cold surfaces can be unhealthy, to say the least.

OPTIONS:

Ogres to Ogre-Mages

Build Time: 250

Gold: 1,000

Research Bloodlust

Build Time: 100

Gold: 1,000

Research Runes

Build Time: 150

Gold: 1,000

Goblin Alchemist

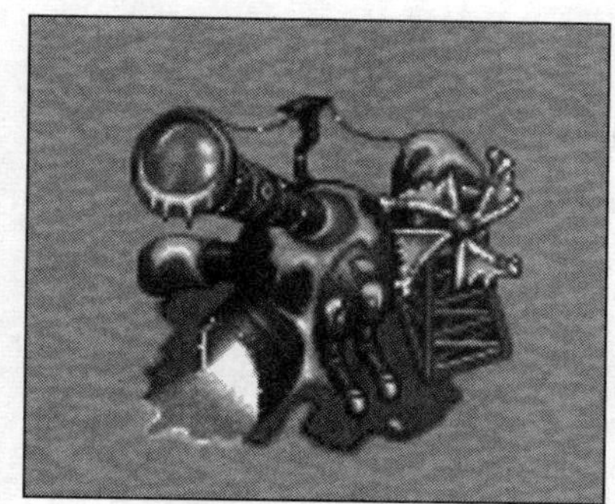

Visual Range:	3
Hit Points:	500
Build Time:	150
Gold Cost:	1,000
Lumber Cost:	400
Armor:	20

The maniacal and brilliant Goblin Alchemists are masters of volatile chemicals, explosives, and obscure mechanical devices. Having constructed Zeppelins to soar above the battlefield and watertight pilot-shacks for use on the enslaved race of giant Sea Turtles, the Goblins have defied the very laws of nature. The Alchemists take a peculiar delight in these intellectual endeavors; few understand them, but all in the Horde respect the havoc that they produce.

Options:

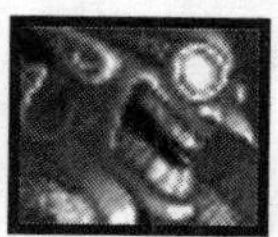

Build Goblin Zeppelin

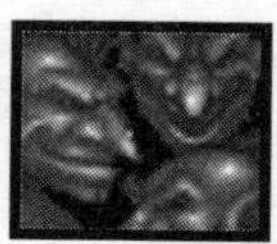

Train Goblin Sappers

Temple of the Damned

Visual Range:	3
Hit Points:	500
Build Time:	125
Gold Cost:	1,000
Lumber Cost:	200
Armor:	20

Temples of the Damned—called *Grombolar* in the Orcish tongue, meaning *bowels of the giant*—are the dwellings of the dead. Created by Gul'dan to house his blasphemous Death Knights, the Temples were formed from the petrified carcasses of the race of giants that inhabited the Orcish homeworld. The subterranean labyrinth of the Temple contains the fetid halls where the Death Knights dwell. There, the Death Knights study their depraved necromancy by practicing it on fallen warriors harvested from the battlefields above.

Options:

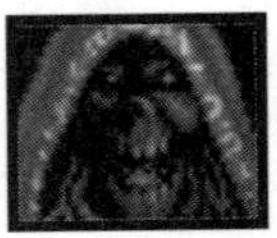

Train Death Knight

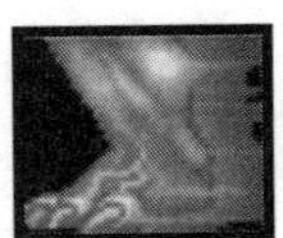

Research Haste

Build Time: 100

Gold: 500

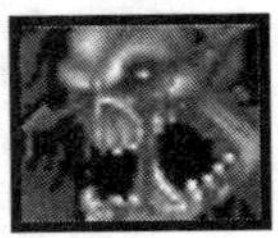

Research Raise Dead

Build Time: 100

Gold: 1,500

Research Whirlwind

Build Time: 150

Gold: 1,500

Research Unholy Armor

Build Time: 200

Gold: 2,500

Research Death and Decay

Build Time: 200

Gold: 2,000

Dragon Roost

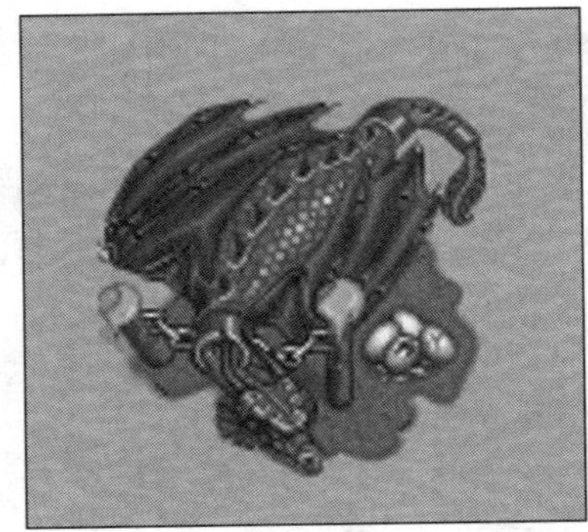

Visual Range:	3
Hit Points:	500
Build Time:	150
Gold Cost:	1,000
Lumber Cost:	400
Armor:	20

Mighty chains of adamantine steel bind the most powerful creature in all of Azeroth: Alexstrasza, the Dragon Queen. Captured and ensorceled by magicks contrived by the Dragonmaw clan, the great Dragon is kept in a constant state of weakness and pain. As the unwilling slave of the Horde, the Queen is closely watched as she lays her precious eggs. The Dragonmaw clan then raises her young to fight for the Horde; her whelps are slayed when they become too powerful to be properly controlled. Constant efforts are made to break Alexstrasza's will so that her captors can master the control of more mature Dragons.

Options:

Build Dragon

Shipyard

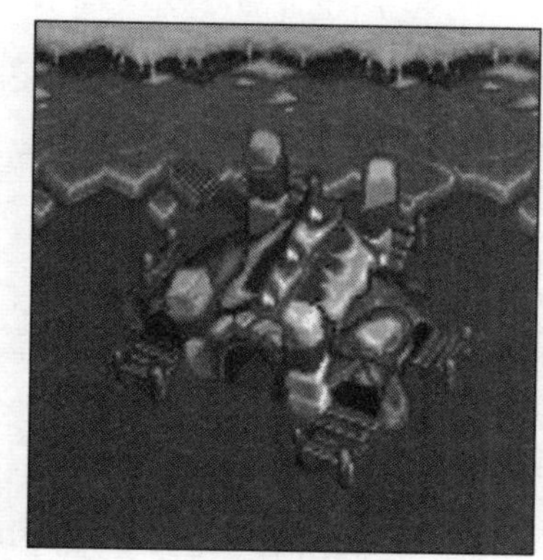

Visual Range:	3
Hit Points:	1,100
Build Time:	200
Gold Cost:	800
Lumber Cost:	450
Armor:	20

Although it is a haphazard collection of stone, mortar, and cheap lumber, the shabby Orc Shipyard is perhaps the most important structure in the Horde's war effort. As the construction sites for Warships, Transports, and Tankers, Shipyards are vital links among the clans scattered across Lordaeron. These sites also have crude processing facilities, so Tankers can deliver shipments of oil to them. The Shipyards are manned by procrastinating, slovenly Orcs, who somehow manage to keep production and maintenance on schedule.

Options:

Build Oil Tanker

Build Destroyer

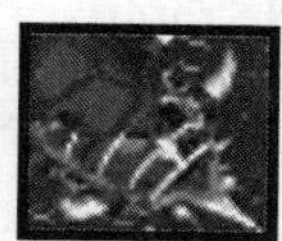

Build Transport

Requires Foundry

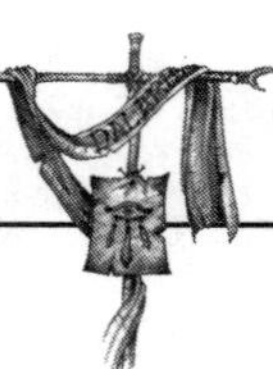

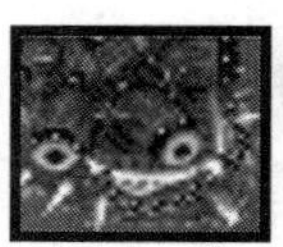

Build Juggernaught

Requires Foundry

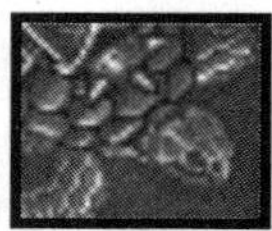

Build Giant Turtle

Requires Goblin Alchemist

Foundry

Visual Range:	3
Hit Points:	750
Build Time:	175
Gold Cost:	700
Lumber Cost:	400
Oil Cost:	400
Armor:	20

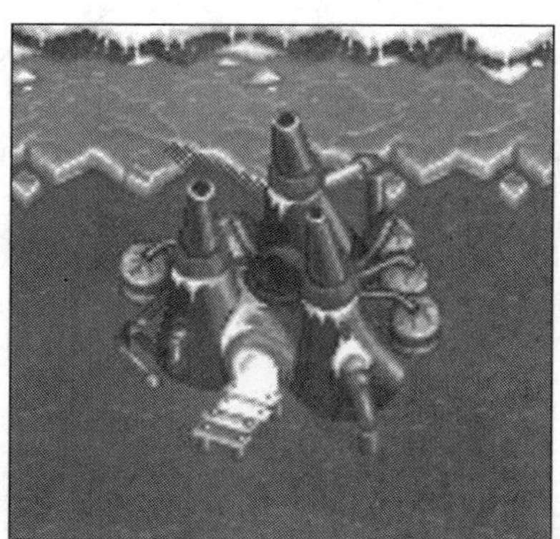

Known by the trio of towering smokestacks that surround it, the Foundry is instrumental in creating the massive armor plates and lethal cannons of the greatest Orc warship—the Juggernaught. Abysmally dark and oppressive with their unnatural heat, Foundries are filled with an acrid layer of smoke and soot—which makes most Orcs feel right at home when visiting one. Heat emanates from all openings as Foundry workers pour molten slag into casts for new cannons, while pounding resounds for miles along the coasts as they shape ore into new armor.

Options:

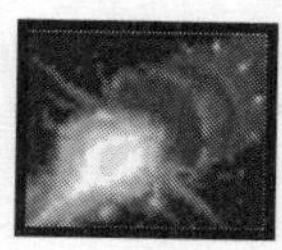

Upgrade Ship Cannons 1

Damage +5

Build Time: 200

Gold: 700

Lumber: 100

Oil: 1,000

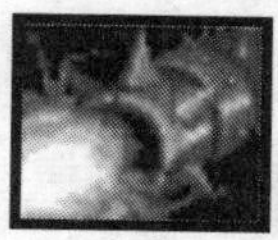

Upgrade Ship Cannons 2

Damage +5

Build Time: 250

Gold: 2,000

Lumber: 250

Oil: 3,000

Upgrade Ship Armor 1

Armor +5

Build Time: 200

Gold: 500

Lumber: 500

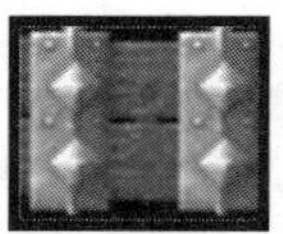

Upgrade Ship Armor 2

Armor +5

Build Time: 250

Gold: 1,500

Lumber: 900

Oil Refinery

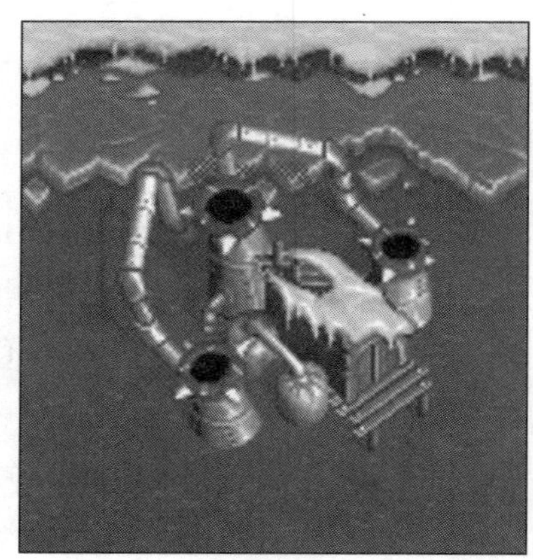

Hit Points:	600
Build Time:	225
Gold Cost:	800
Lumber Cost:	350
Oil Cost:	200
Armor:	20
Production:	Oil 100+25

The Oil Refinery uses the large, arching pipelines on either side of the main structure to pump oil from the Tankers into its processing holds. Built on the rim of the sea, Refineries are constantly threatened by attacks from water-borne vessels. Because a Refinery processes oil much more efficiently than a Shipyard alone, the sight of warships deployed for the defense of these structures is a common one.

Oil Platform

Visual Range:	3
Hit Points:	650
Build Time:	200
Gold Cost:	700
Lumber Cost:	450
Armor:	20

The vast amounts of oil beneath the sea must be used for the construction of ships and various war machines. Because the oceans are rich with this substance, Tankers need to construct platforms where the oil is thick. Only then can the Tankers collect their dark cargo. As the Horde drew near Lordaeron and the seas became increasingly treacherous, the Platforms built by Human drillers before the Great War were destroyed.

METZEN · 95

Chapter Three

The Annals of the Great Alliance

I am Milan of the Elven House of Scribes. I have been given the supreme honor of inscribing these Annals in preparation for the impending invasion by the Orcish Horde. For the first time in our long history, the Great Alliance of Lordaeron has brought together Humans, Elves, Dwarves, and Gnomes under the same banner to remove our common enemy from the face of this world. At this time, I know not whether these Annals will describe our victory or our miserable defeat, but it is my hope

that our ancestors will read and learn from these pages, whatever the outcome. It is for this reason that I am concentrating on the military aspects of our endeavors—so that future leaders may study and expand on them in the event of our demise. The preservation of knowledge is of paramount importance, for the Horde comes to destroy all we have learned and all we love about these lands. I have sworn a great oath to the Alliance to protect these words with my life and to pass this knowledge on to all who would gain the smallest wisdom from it. Tomorrow, I travel to Hillsbrad to record the maps, orders, and tactics of our most promising Human commander. May the Gods favor us. . . .

Act I: The Shores of Lordaeron

Mission One: Hillsbrad

Orders: Because of your position as regional commander of the southern defense forces, Lord Terenas orders you to raise an outpost in the Hillsbrad foothills. It is rumored that Orcish marauders have been raiding coastal towns in the area, but whether these attacks are part of a greater Horde offensive is, as yet, unknown.

Your outpost is to provide food and information for Alliance troops and, therefore, should be a community consisting of at least four Farms. You must also construct a Barracks in order to safeguard the Hillsbrad operation. Your base will give advanced warning of Orcish troop movements in the area; it is an essential part of securing Alliance operations.

Objective: Build four Farms and a Barracks.

Even Peasants can gang up and kill an enemy.

Mission One: Hillsbrad

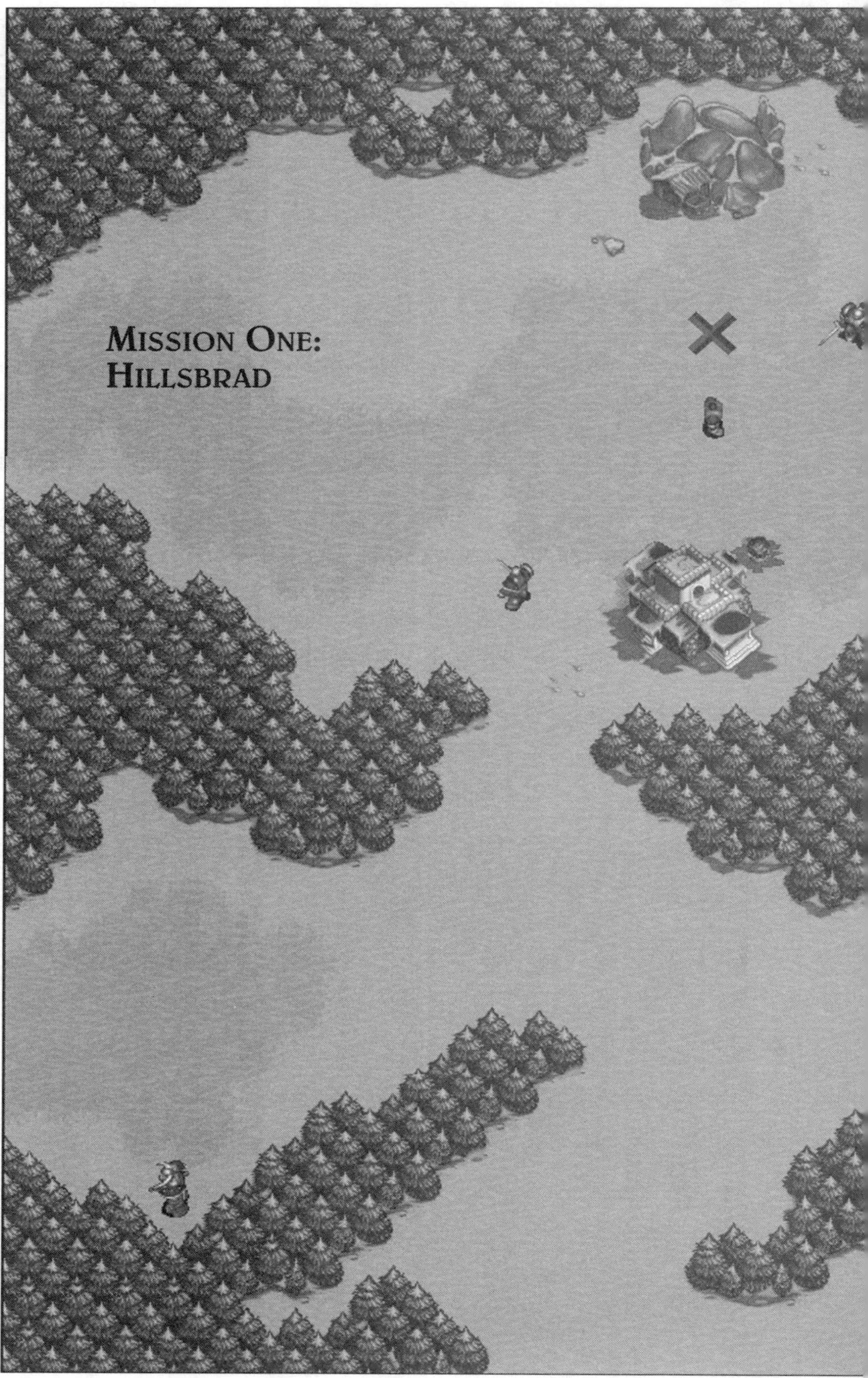

Opening Maneuvers: We have converted a large stone mansion into a Town Hall; the owner has graciously provided his servants and his Farm to assist us as well. Our first task was to plow more farmland for the arrival of more troops, while at the same time training more servants in the ways of construction and mining. An old mine, nearby to the north, was reopened after the second Farm was completed, and all available workers helped gather the necessary materials for building. The forest was strangely quiet today. Our units of Footmen stayed close to the Hall.

Carrying Out Our Orders: As soon as the workers had extracted all they could from the mine, we immediately began the construction of a Barracks. We have received word of coming reinforcements, so all the local Peasants helped build from the outside at the same time the interior was being completed in an effort to finish before their arrival. With that task completed all that remained was to cut enough lumber for two more Farms. The workers are staying near the edge of the tree line; our troops continue to closely guard our efforts.

Securing the Area: Today the completion of the Farms heralded the arrival of reinforcements, who brought grim news of battles to the south and the presence of several bands of Orcs nearby. With our task completed and preparations for war begun, we decided to remain where we were and enjoy the quiet until we received new orders.

Mission Two: Ambush at Tarren Mill

Orders: The High Command has sent word that the Elves of Silvermoon have sent a contingent of Archers south to survey the supposed Orcish threat for themselves. Unfortunately, our spies report that shortly after passing through the Alterac grasslands the Elves were ambushed by Horde troops. It is believed that these Elves are now being held in a small prison camp near the northwest region of Tarren Mill.

Lord Terenas, fervently hoping to enlist more Elves into the Alliance, has asked you to form a party to hunt for the missing Elves and lead them to safety. As a sign of good faith, the Elves have sent a cadre of Archers to assist you in your search. You will also be provided with plans to construct an Elven Lumber Mill and the sylvan craftsmen to operate it.

Objective: Find and rescue at least one Elven Archer and return him to the Circle of Power inside your base.

Opening Maneuvers: We arrived at Tarren Mill with a stalwart group of Footmen, and were greeted by Elven Archers who had already prepared the village for war. They had also located our captured brethren to the northwest, and were armed and ready to seek revenge. The enemy camp was too far inland for our warships to assist, so we made preparations to march. We briefly considered training more soldiers for the raid, but the Archers were eager to spill Orcish blood and convinced us to strike at dawn.

Carrying Out Our Orders: Still fatigued from yesterday's march, we gathered around the Circle of Power at first light and prepared our weapons.

Spies reported that many of the Orcs had spread out to plunder the surrounding area, leaving a minimal guard at the unorganized outpost. We headed north and northwest in a tight group, wary of anything that moved. Startled Orcs and Trolls sent up war cries, but our force easily outnumbered them and slew them one at a time.

We then quickly returned through the village and headed west to approach the camp from the south, out of range of the Guard Tower. More foul beasts were felled on the way, and when we entered the clearing south of the camp, the guards came howling out after us as expected. We led them further south and killed those who did not turn back. This we repeated until all the guards had been dispatched; then we rushed the Tower as a group. Before we had time to destroy it, a deep horn sounded an alarm, and we had very little time to break through a section of wall and get inside before the remaining Orcs returned. Once inside, our Archers tossed bows and quivers to the captives. We stood our ground inside until all was quiet.

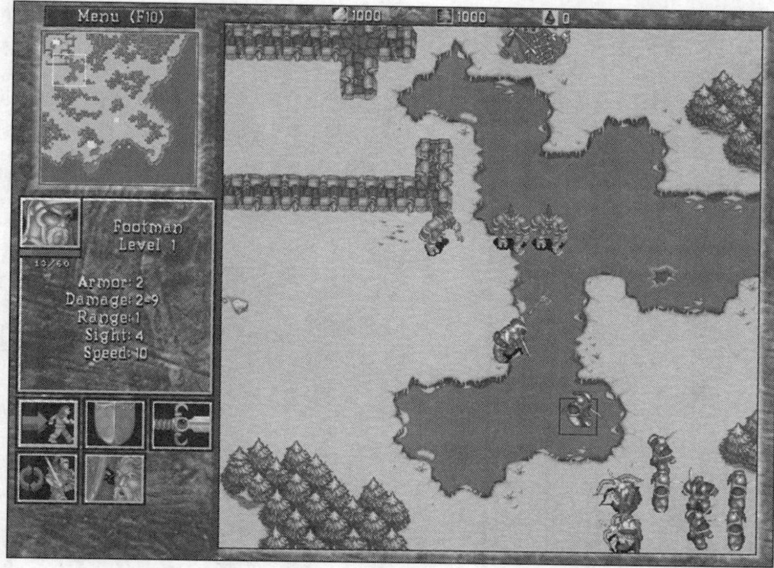

Lead bloodthirsty Orcs and Trolls away from their defenses.

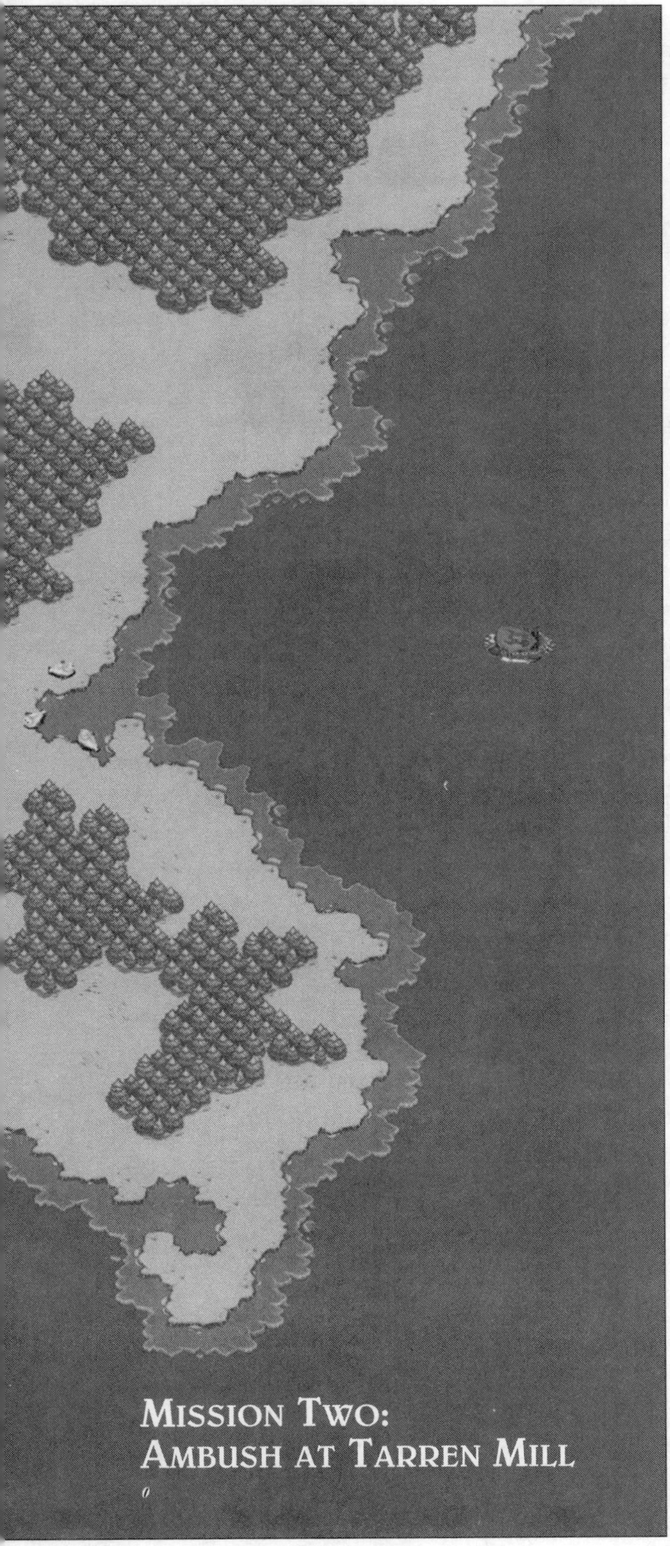

Securing the Area: Cold and bleeding, our victorious group returned to Tarren Mill and immediately sent word of our success. Not a single Orc remained in the forest; enemy ships nearby were quickly sunk to prevent further problems. The reclusive Elves of Silvermoon bade us farewell to return home. I am not certain they will persuade their leaders to join the Alliance. We had but a single night's rest before an Elven Destroyer arrived with orders to board ship and sail to the south, where the sounds of war were becoming commonplace.

Mission Two:
Ambush at Tarren Mill

Mission Three: Southshore

Orders: With the safe return of the Elves from the loathsome clutches of the Orcs, the Council of Silvermoon has resolved to combine the armies of Quel'thalas with those of the Alliance of Lordaeron. As a show of their support, they have sent a mighty fleet of Elven Destroyers to help safeguard the Lordaeron mainland.

In preparation for the arrival of these ships, Daelin Proudmoore—Lord of Kul Tiras and Grand Admiral of the Lordaeron Fleet—has ordered you to begin the construction of naval facilities near the township of Southshore. There is some suspicion that the Horde has constructed a secret base near the mainland, so it is imperative that you begin building your defense with haste.

Objective: Construct at least four Oil Platforms.

Opening Maneuvers: Our first task on arrival was to build another Farm to feed the large number of workers and sailors that would soon arrive. Next, we set the workers to collecting materials from the mine nearby and continued training new Peasants as fast as our resources permitted. The Destroyer on which we had arrived remained in place to guard the shoreline; the soldiers stayed near camp, since spies had confirmed reports of an enemy base offshore. Rather than risk an encounter, we decided to build up as quickly and quietly as possible. Once we had five workers in the mines and a small amount of gold saved up, we constructed a Lumber Mill from the wood on hand and still had enough for another Farm. The troops were unhappy not to have a Barracks, but we were planning a naval assault and, therefore, trained still more workers to gather wood for processing in the new Mill. No enemies had been spotted yet, but we knew they were about.

Carrying Out Our Orders: After several days of gathering lumber, we began construction of the Shipyard on the shore to the east of our camp. On the night before it was completed, a small boat carrying shipwrights and sailors emerged from the mist above the waves. They were lucky to have come through alive. We gladly provided them with whatever building materials they needed, and soon they had christened their first Oil Tanker. It was a

shoddy contraption, held together with pine tar and luck, but it managed to ferry enough supplies to build an Oil Platform nearby to the east. They built a second Tanker soon after, and a steady flow of black gold was soon filling our oak barrels as fast as we could make them. At the same time, more Farms were being built to feed the growing population of workers, who easily outnumbered the troops stationed here. We were all much relieved when construction of new Destroyers began, because we still had not enough time or resources to build a Barracks. With the surplus of workers gathering materials, we built five warships in a matter of weeks.

With this powerful fleet, we first swept along the coastline northeast and nicely exploded a Troll spy. Keeping this in mind, we then swept westward and secured the coast in that direction. At the western edge of the coast, we steered directly south toward the horizon and quickly spotted two enemy Destroyers guarding one of their own Platforms. These we sank effortlessly; we then gave their Platform the same treatment. From there we sailed east and spotted more Destroyers around a small island. Those sank below the waves first; then we opened fire on the structures and enemies on the island. When the smoke from our cannons cleared, all that remained was scattered debris.

Structures close to shore are fair game for warships.

Mission Three: Southshore

Securing the Area: The column of smoke on the horizon prompted the remaining Orcs on the mainland to attempt a raid, but even the few troops guarding the camp were able to stop them. From there it was only a matter of time before we built three more Platforms—just in time for the approaching flotilla of warships that would soon transform our camp into a busy seaport. We were not present to see it, however, since new orders took us elsewhere as usual.

Mission Four: Attack Zul'dare

Orders: Having established some order in the region with a display of naval power, Admiral Proudmoore advises that the time has come to seek out the secret lair of the Orcs. Scouts report that this base is located somewhere within the Zul'dare region of the Channel Islands, just southeast of Hillsbrad. Lordaeron artificers have completed designs for a Refinery that will process oil with greater efficiency. With this new innovation, you will be able to construct Transport ships that can ferry your troops across large bodies of water. These vessels should provide great assistance in the completion of your task.

Objective: Seek out and demolish the Orc base.

Opening Maneuvers: Given the threat of enemy ships nearby, our first priority was to get a Shipyard into operation as soon as possible. First, we sent our worker into the mines for the purpose of training more. At the same time, the two Destroyers that had brought us here were sent from the northern shore around to the south where an enemy Destroyer guarded an oil patch. When it was safely below the waves, they remained near the shore to guard the Shipyard site.

After training several more Peasants, we placed half of them in the mines and set the other half to collecting lumber. Soon we raised a Lumber Mill and, soon after, began construction of the Shipyard on the southern shore near camp. Taking no chances, we also constructed a Barracks to train a force of Archers for the coming amphibious assault. Though we were still training Peasants and building Farms, there was more than enough material and sufficient laborers to start the Refinery and Foundry. Meanwhile, new Tankers began exploiting the nearby patch of oil.

Carrying Out Our Orders: With all the necessary structures in place and operational, we next began preparations for war. We raised Guard Towers on the north shore to fend off landing raiders and spent time upgrading our arrows, ship cannons, and armor. More Destroyers were necessary to clear the way for our Transports, which were constructed only after we already

had five Destroyers in the water. During this time, we continually trained new Archers until there were ten units, which easily defended the camp until the Transports that would carry them were completed.

Our fleet of Destroyers began the operation by sailing south and southeast, directly into enemy territory. We kept them together and eliminated enemy craft one at a time; owing to this strategy, soon there was little opposition to our reducing the platforms and coastal structures to piles of smoking ash. With that completed, we anchored the Destroyers close to shore near the enemy camp and let them fire at Orcs for sport while the Transports were being loaded with ten Archers and two Peasants. Once they had landed safely just west of our Destroyers, the Archers made sure our workers could construct two Guard Towers directly north of the Destroyers. We were very careful not to let our Archers wander into the camp, keeping them close to the Towers and Destroyers for defense. Once the Guard Towers were in place and upgraded, next came a Barracks, whose completion spelled doom for the vile Orcs.

Clear the way for an invasion with artillery support.

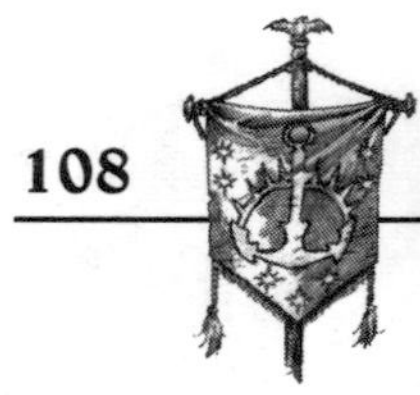

Mission Four: Attack Zul'dare

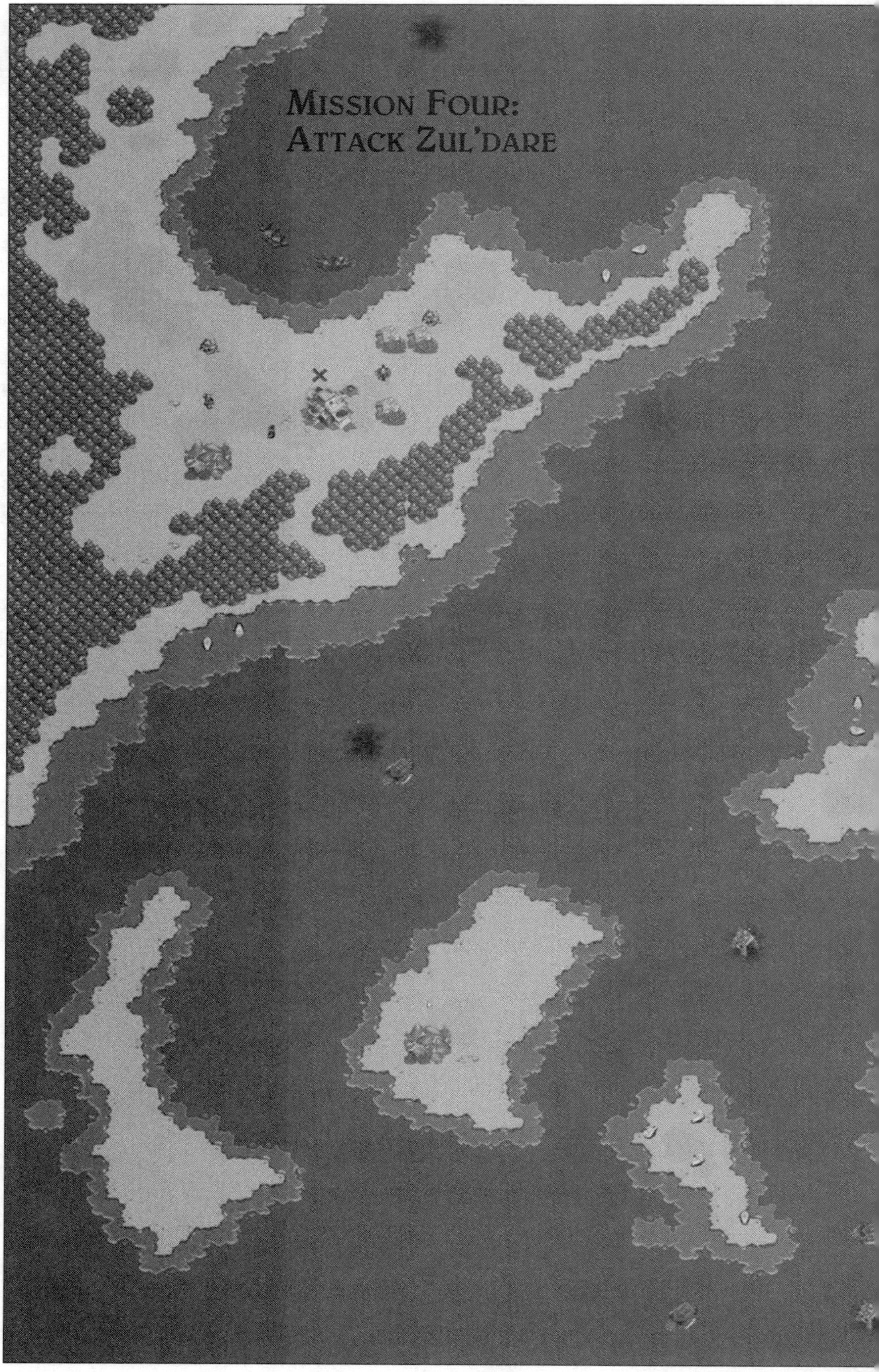

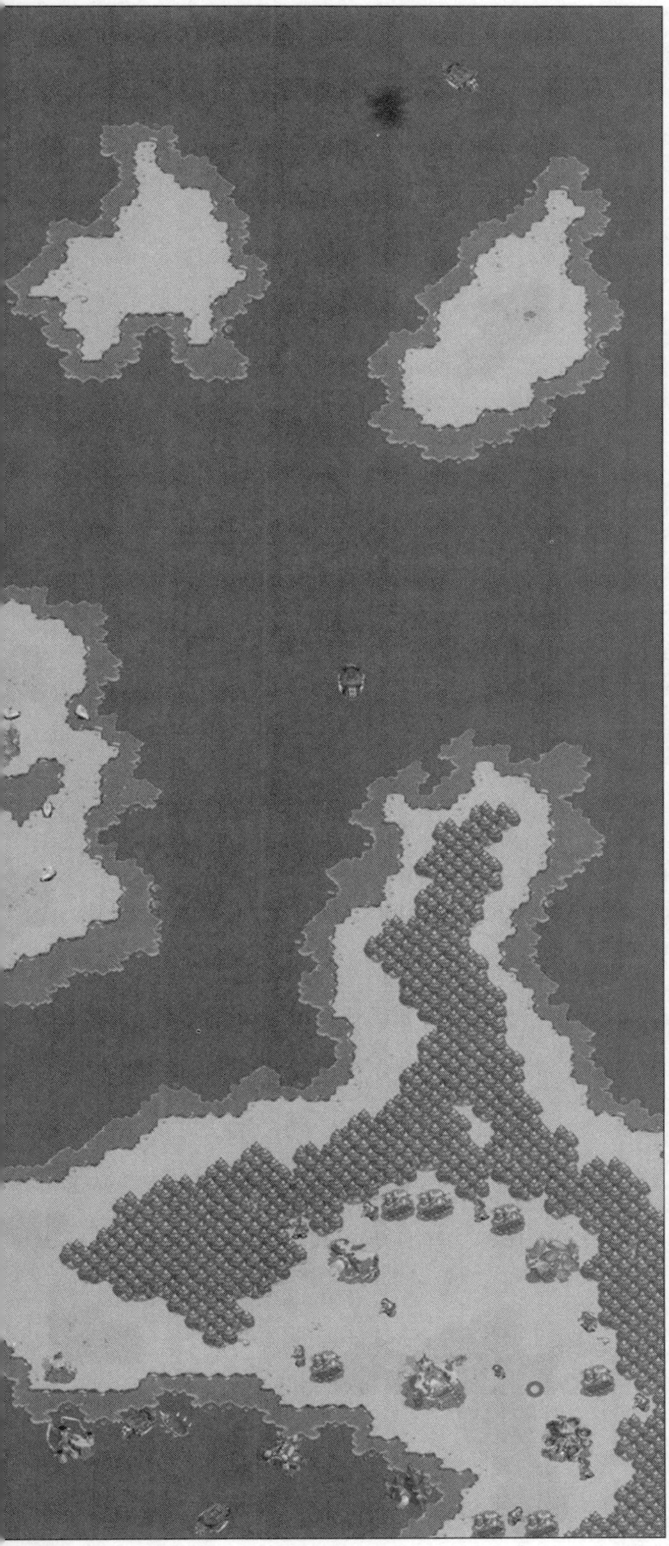

SECURING THE AREA: While we were cleaning out the enemy camp, the remaining enemy ships in the area decided to try for our home base. They were soundly defeated by the Guard Towers we had constructed along the shore. We then sought out and killed the few remaining Orcs, and celebrated our victory among the ruins, which still burned and smoked angrily. Today was a great triumph for the Alliance; our skill in battle earned us a trip to the heart of the war on the mainland to the north.

Act II: Khaz Modan

Mission Five: Tol Barad

Orders: Impressed by your series of victories against the Horde and by the destruction of the Zul'dare base, the High Command has decided to dispatch you and your troops to the main battleground. The forces of Stromgarde and Kul Tiras are currently stationed along the northern border of Khaz Modan, fighting to keep the Orcs from advancing into southern Lordaeron. An Orcish outpost, nestled near the ruins of the ancient Dwarven city of Dun Modr, has repeatedly beaten back Alliance troops and ravaged the surrounding farmlands. You must reclaim the nearby island Keep at Tol Barad and then launch an attack on the Horde outpost at Dun Modr.

Objective: Reclaim Tol Barad and destroy the Orc Base at Dun Modr.

Opening Maneuvers: As we rushed to board the waiting Transports, we could already see smoke rising from the nearby island. We sailed toward it, on the northeast side, and landed just in time to interrupt the demolition of a Barracks there. Several of our number died in the attack, but we were able to slaughter the Orcs and Trolls before they could finish their foul deed. Once we were safely inside the camp, the grateful inhabitants were eager to follow our orders, and soon the Barracks was repaired while we raised Cannon Towers behind it to prevent further destruction. With all the structures intact, we then built more Farms and trained workers to speed our efforts. On the western shore of the island we began a Shipyard, while the Tanker that accompanied us found an oil patch a short distance further west and proceeded to build a Platform over it. We were soon ready to begin building Ballistas for our lightning strike on the Orc-infested island to the northeast.

Carrying Out Our Orders: Within days, we had assembled our amphibious force near the Shipyard and had loaded the Transports with six Ballistas, five Archers, and one Peasant. Escorted by Destroyers, we launched and sailed for the west side of the enemy base. We sank a single enemy

Destroyer on the way, while the rest of their fleet was busy guarding the other side. After landing, the worker we had brought quickly began a Tower on the closest patch of flat ground. With a line of trees obscuring the Orcs' view of our operation, we were able to construct two Cannon Towers and a makeshift Barracks unmolested. This temporary base was a testament to the inherent aggressiveness of Orcs, for they were very cooperative when we sent a single Archer to greet them and lead the howling monsters back within range of our waiting forces. Shortly thereafter, we began the assault on their base by land, a stratagem for which they were obviously unprepared.

SECURING THE AREA: After leveling most of their structures, we lined up our Ballistas along the shoreline and sank the majority of their ships. Those that remained were removed by a second group of our Destroyers; we finished the operation by hunting down and slaughtering all of the panicked Orcs that were left. It was a complete success; news of our victory quickly spread to the mainland.

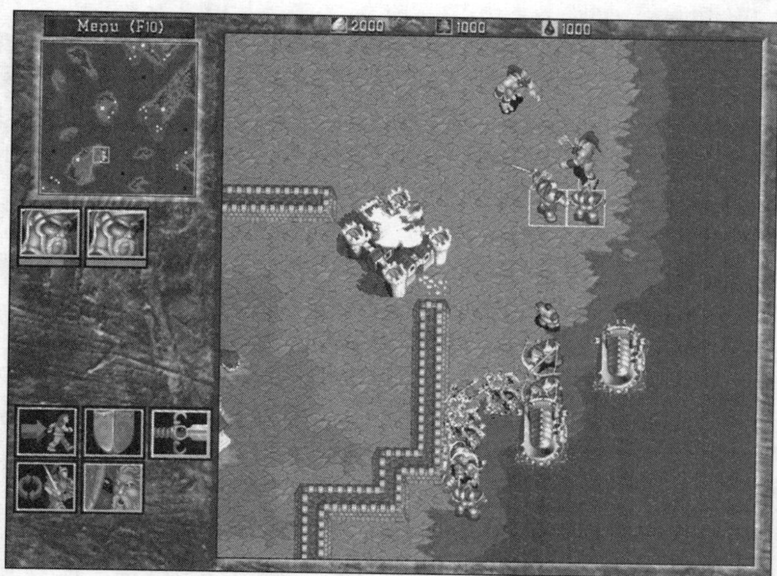

Land quickly to save the Barracks.

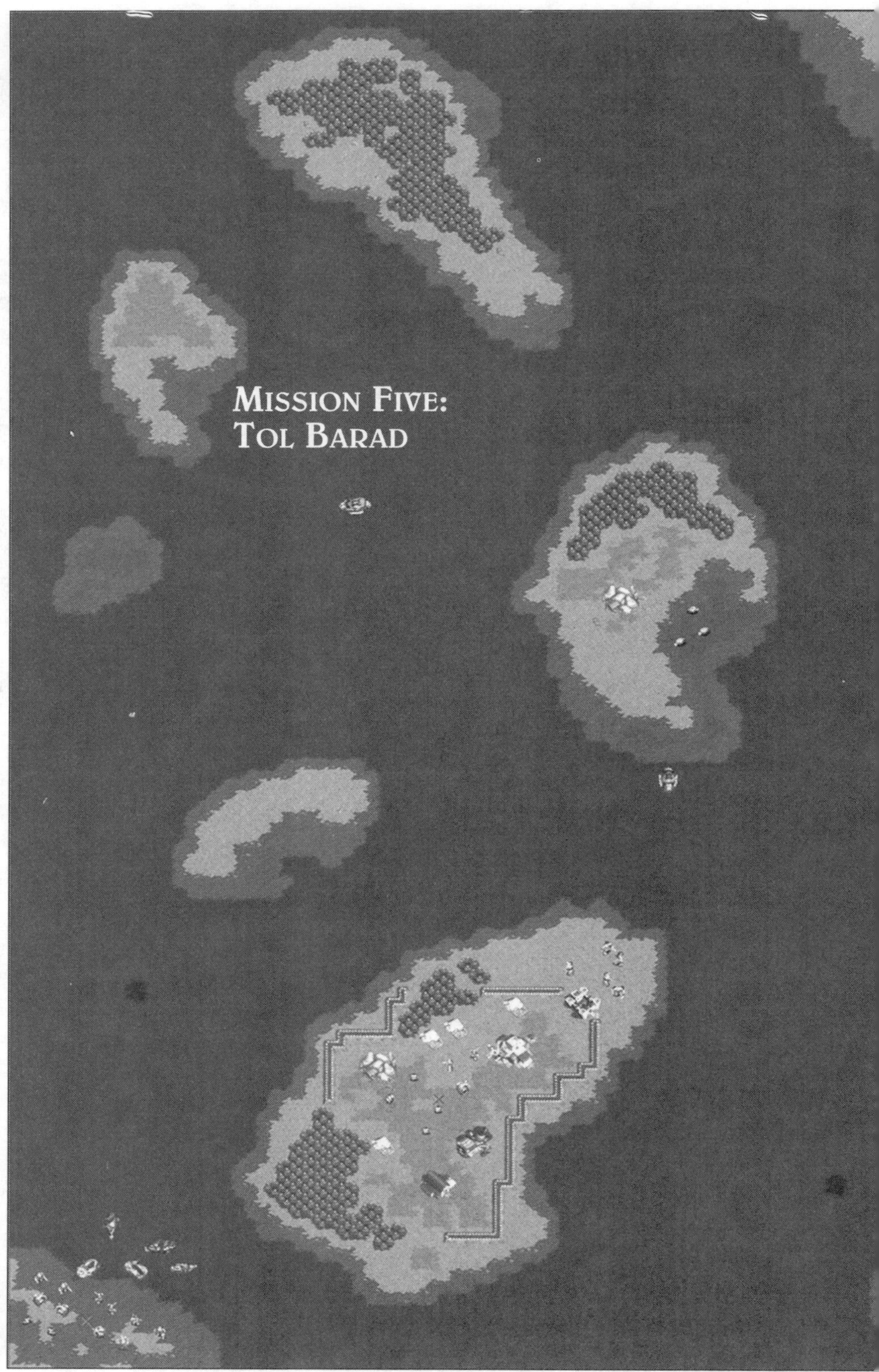
MISSION FIVE:
TOL BARAD

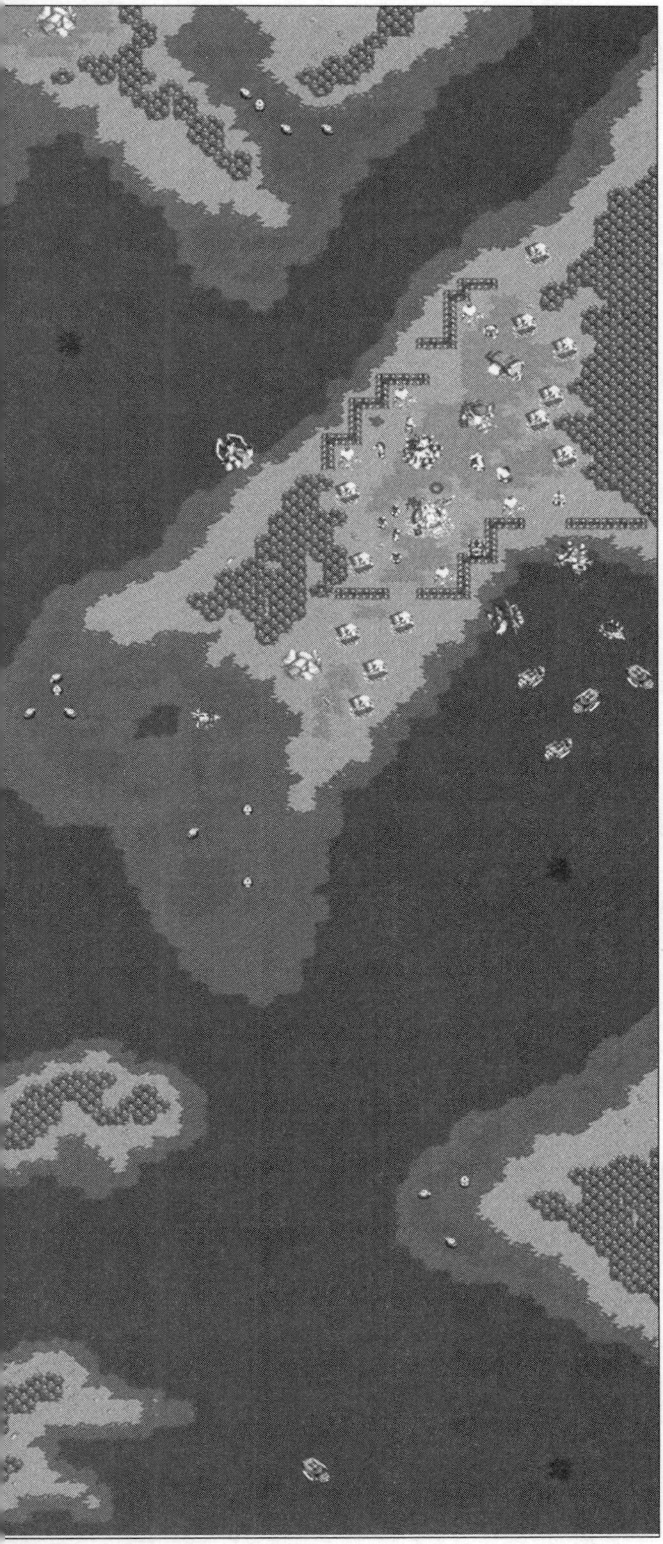

Mission Six: Dun Algaz

Orders: Following their defeat at Dun Modr, the Orcs were forced to retreat south, across the Thandol Valley to a secondary outpost at Dun Algaz. Lord Lothar, hoping to push the Orcs even further back into Khaz Modan, has ordered you to destroy this newly discovered encampment. A small company of Knights has been placed under your command by Lothar to aid you in your mission.

Objective: Destroy Dun Algaz.

Opening Maneuvers: Our first task was to train more Peasants to plunder the nearby mine, for we would need its contents for the coming land raid. Our force would consist mostly of Knights and Ballistas, so a Blacksmith was required as well as a Keep. We also built Cannon Towers at the eastern and western openings of the base to fend off occasional raids by Orcs. Although we had the research and training available for Rangers, our commander was confident that Knights would be more suitable for the attack, and we spent much time and resources enhancing their weapons and armor.

Carrying Out Our Orders: The attacking force gathered just outside camp. It consisted of nine proud Knights and three Ballistas for heavy artillery. Scouts have located three narrow land bridges leading to the enemy; we chose the most direct route, down the center one. The Knights rode in front of the slower war machines, occasionally waiting for them. As we neared the end of the land bridge, a large party of mixed Horde monsters attacked, but they were no match for our great mounted warriors.

Close to the south, we spotted a makeshift enemy Barracks and promptly leveled it. Then we summoned a few Peasants from our home camp and set them to work on our own temporary Barracks on the same spot, while our Knights stood guard impatiently. For good measure, we also built Cannon Towers on both sides of the Barracks and, with those completed, sent the workers back home.

Securing the Area: One of our Knights was sent toward the enemy to lure them out; our Ballistas made quick work of their Towers after most of the defenders were dead. From this point, it was only a matter of demolition and slaughter as new Knights and Ballistas emerged from the makeshift Barracks to replace those lost in battle. For the first time in months, all of us were feeling hope that the Horde could be stopped, but the road to final victory would be long.

Destroy the enemy Barracks to make room for your own in enemy territory.

Mission Six: Dun Algaz

Mission Seven: Grim Batol

Orders: Advance scouts report that they have located Grim Batol—the primary base of the Horde's Refinery operations in Khaz Modan. Seeing a chance to strike a decisive blow against the Horde, Lord Lothar has ordered you to infiltrate Grim Batol and put an end to all Orcish activity there.

Lothar believes that once Grim Batol has been destroyed, the Orcs will have no further use for Khaz Modan and will therefore pull their forces back to the mainland of Azeroth. Victory could secure the shores of Lordaeron and greatly impede the Horde offensive.

Objective: Destroy five Oil Refineries.

Opening Maneuvers: We landed as close to Grim Batol as possible. From there we would have to march south, leaving the workers and Transports behind for safety. As we proceeded, we were disturbed to discover two enemy Catapults, fortified behind a wall and guarded by several Orcs. Swearing oaths to all the Gods, we steeled ourselves and rushed directly toward them. The Gods heard our prayers that day for the Catapults were unmanned, and after killing the guards, we broke through the wall and claimed them for ourselves. Continuing south, we destroyed an enemy Tower with their own war machines and claimed yet another Catapult for ourselves. Only then did we summon the Transports and Peasants south to join us, following which our force boarded ship to land on the other side of the river. This time we swept northward, careful to remove enemy Towers with the Catapults, and soon leveled all the foul Orcish structures so that we could raise our own.

Carrying Out Our Orders: We quickly erected a Town Hall near a mine to the north and began collecting resources. Our commander was planning to build Battleships for the attack, so a Lumber Mill and a Shipyard were needed as soon as possible. While the Shipyard was being built, we decided to place a Refinery at the southeastern tip of a small peninsula, conveniently

near an oil patch. After Tankers had been built to exploit it, a Foundry was raised near the Shipyard, which provided the heavy cannons and armor for Battleships. Unfortunately, the mine was running dry, so we built a Transport to ferry workers across to another nearby mine and a temporary Town Hall near it to collect the resources. Finally, construction of the Battleships began; we spent our extra time and gold to develop better cannons and armor to ensure their success.

Securing the Area: At last we had six tall Battleships with which to attack, and sailed them south into enemy territory. They made quick work of the enemy vessels that tried to stop them. Ignoring the Oil Platforms and Refineries for a time, we then concentrated on removing the Towers and Catapults that guarded them. As the Horde watched helplessly, we began pounding their structures; soon they were forced to surrender to our might.

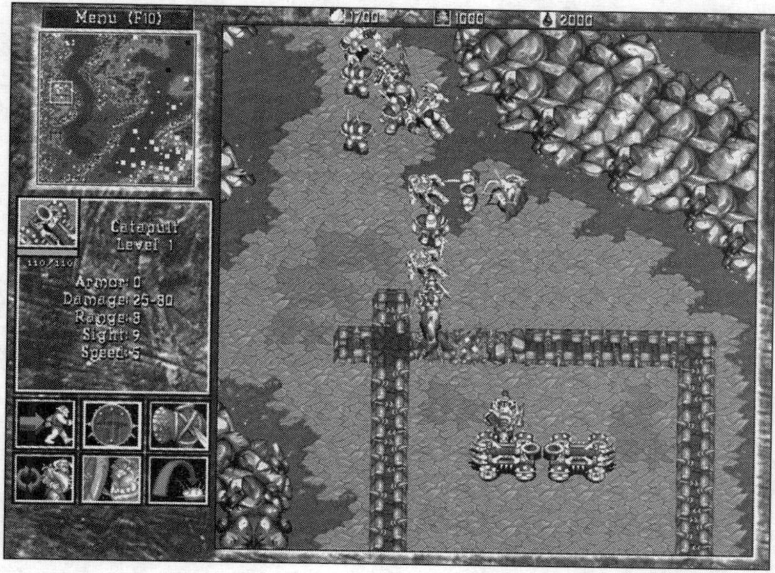

Capture unmanned enemy Catapults for your own use.

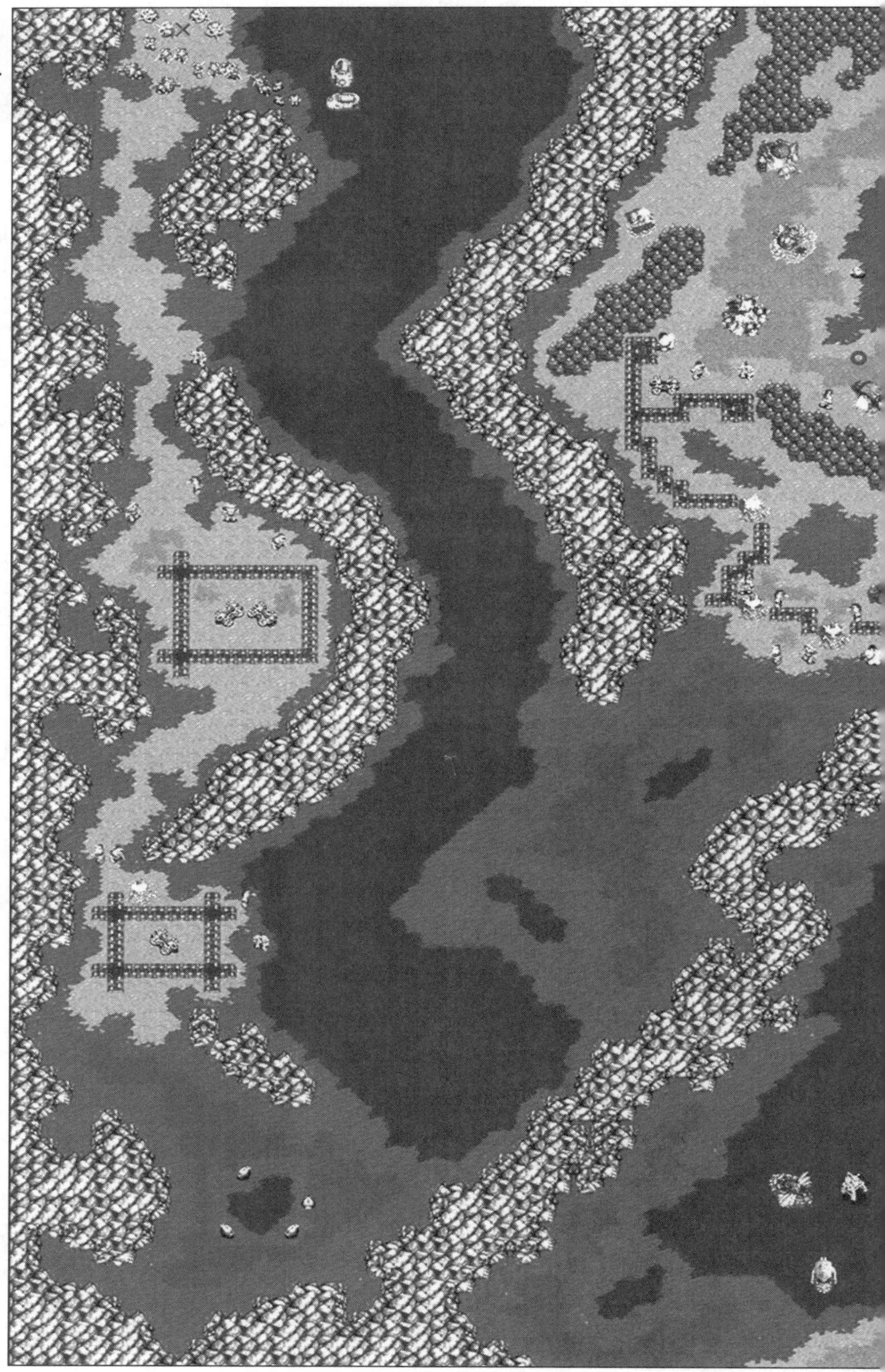

Mission Seven: Grim Batol

Act III: The Northlands

Mission Eight: Tyr's Hand

Orders: With the destruction of Dun Modr and the downfall of the Oil Refinery at Grim Batol, the Orcs have completely withdrawn their armies from Khaz Modan. Although your victories have been notable, the menace of the Horde still hangs over the Alliance. Lord Lothar has stationed your troops in the northlands to protect the borders of Quel'thalas.

Troubles have arisen in the township of Tyr's Hand; the local Peasant population is in a state of minor revolt. You must quell this uprising and then summon the Knights of the Silver Hand to hearten and watch over the populace. Once peace has been restored, determine whether there is Orcish activity in the region. If you encounter any Horde forces, they are to be intercepted and routed.

Objective: Quell the peasant uprising in Tyr's Hand, construct a secondary Castle in the northwest to maintain order in the region, and destroy all enemy forces.

Opening Maneuvers: Slaughtering Human workers was unpleasant, but with the Horde nearby, this action was necessary to ensure our survival. Once the township was quiet, we had very little time to make preparations for war. We trained more Peasants to speed mining operations while our troops patrolled inside the town walls, ever vigilant for raiding Orcs. Barracks were constructed first, and then a Lumber Mill near the forests on the east side of town. Next came the transformation of the Town Hall into a Keep. To protect our efforts, we constructed Farms to block the north and west entrances. Behind these we raised Cannon Towers, placing Archers near them for good measure. The remaining troops were gathered near the other entrances while Stables were prepared for the arriving Paladins.

Carrying Out Our Orders: Once the township had been properly fortified, we began training Knights and constructing Catapults for the coming battles. When resources were available, the Keep was fortified into a stalwart Castle and a Church was constructed for the Paladins, who invited our Knights to join them and learn their craft. To ensure their success, we spent much time and gold preparing better weapons, armor, and Ballista spears in the Smithy. Ten Paladins and four Ballistas gathered in the courtyard before sallying out, and the long process of cleaning out Orcs began in earnest.

Securing the Area: We sent a single Paladin northward to draw enemies toward a row of Ballistas defended by Paladins. Though many of the creatures turned back, a few were aggressive enough to fall into the trap. This we repeated until the number of guards in the northern camp was greatly reduced. Only then did we roll in the Ballistas to help take out structures.

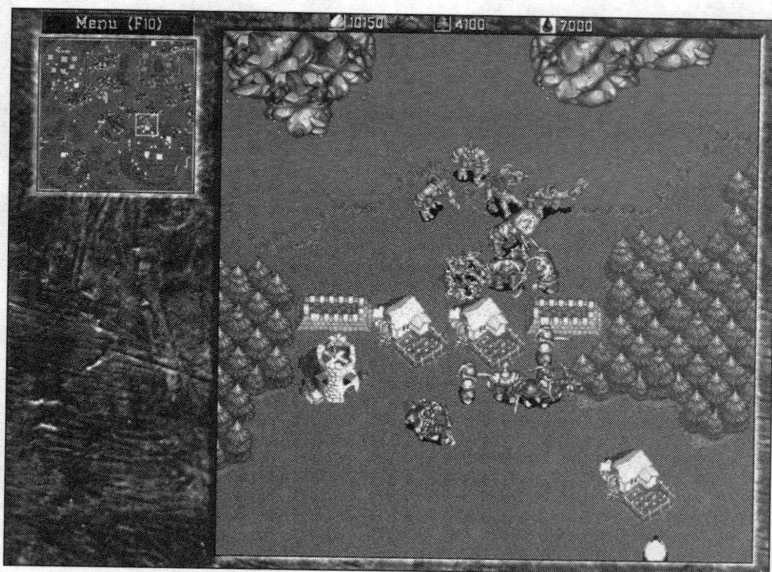

Build Farms and Towers to block entrances.

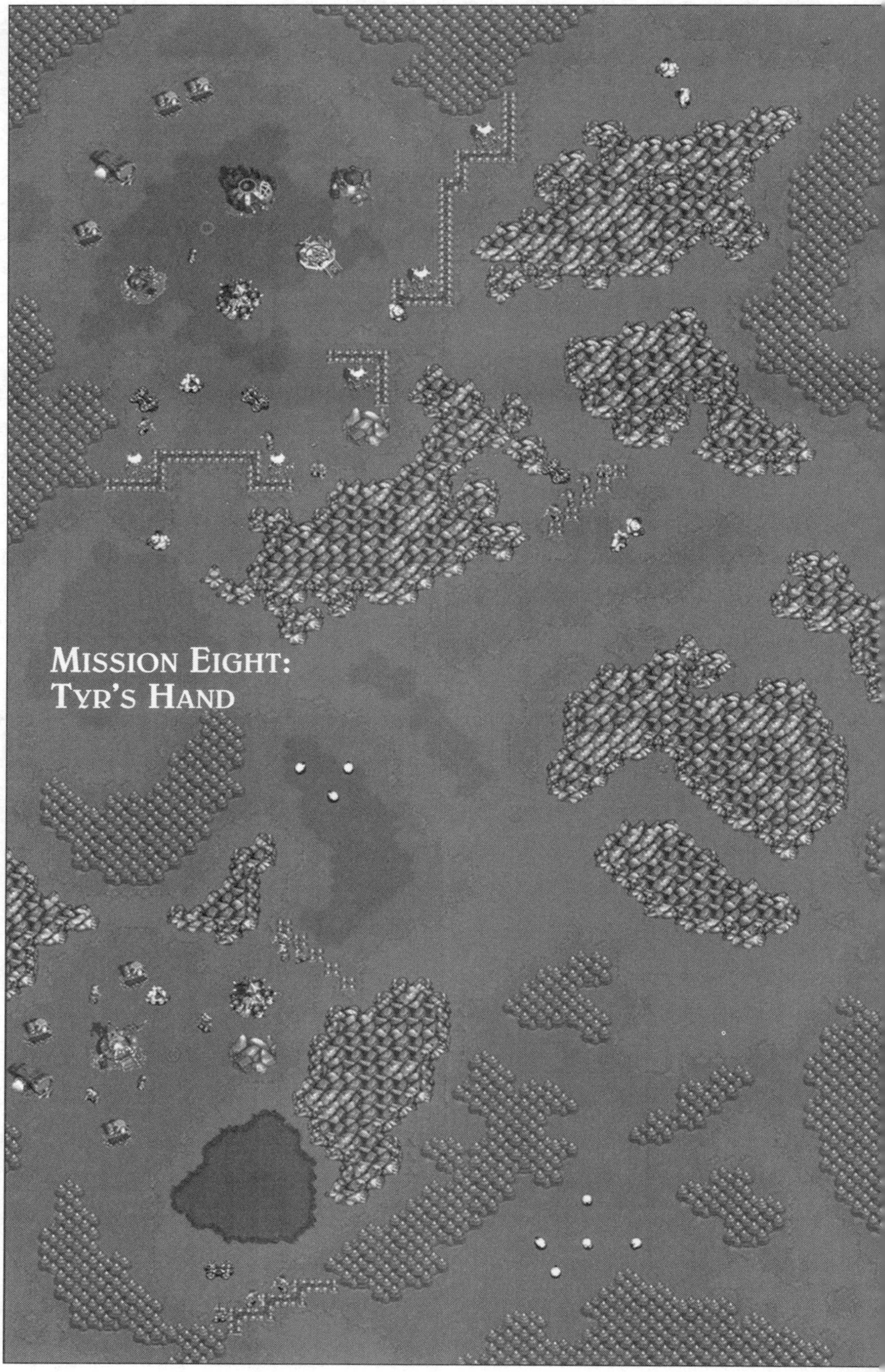

Mission Eight: Tyr's Hand

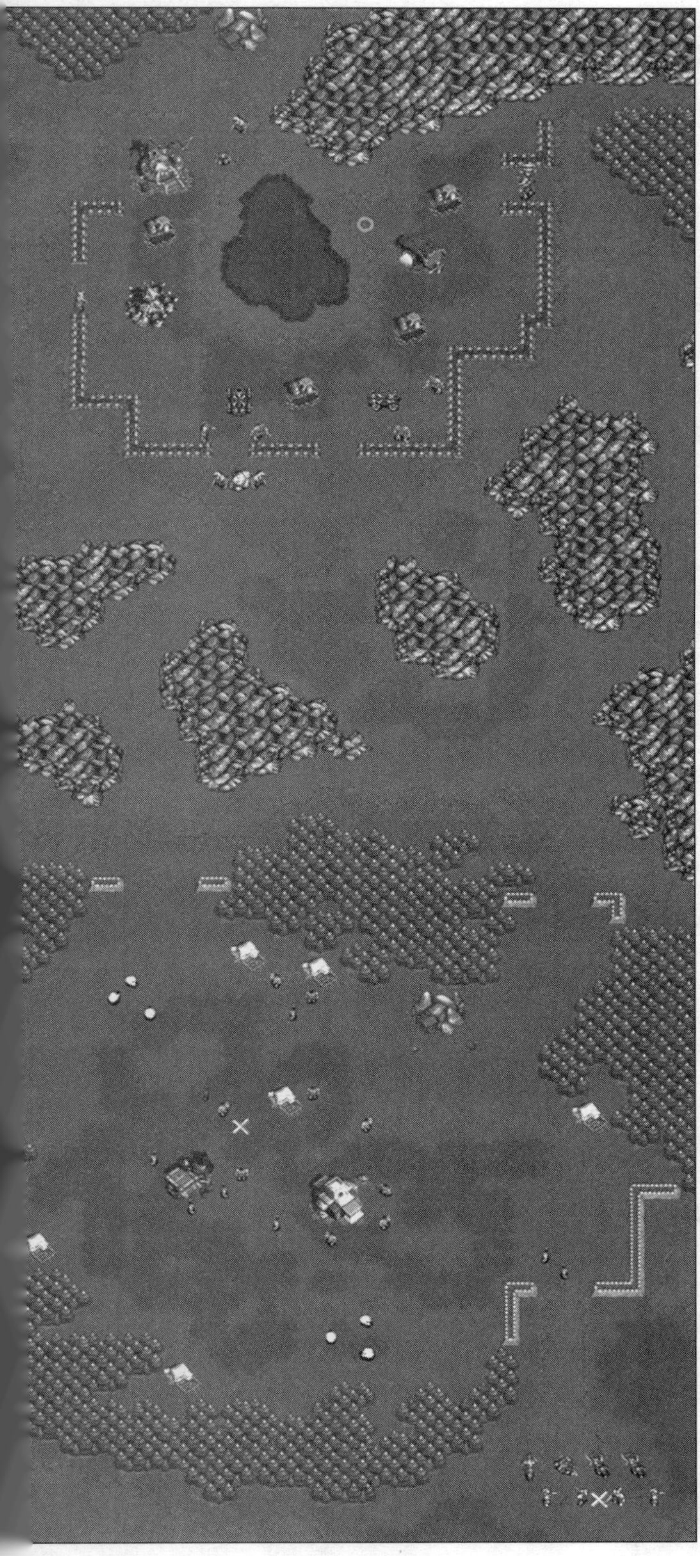

Several raids were made on our township, but our fortifications held nicely with Cannon Towers defending them. We then started destroying the camp to the west of town, replacing fallen warriors as needed. Finally, we assembled a large force of mixed units to remove the stronger threat to the northwest and, with that task completed, constructed a second Castle on the ruins to prevent further problems here. The Horde was now on the defensive and the ground was soaked with Orcish blood rather than our own.

Mission Nine: The Battle at Darrowmere

Orders: With his Paladins keeping vigilant watch over the northlands, the Archbishop's assistant Uther Lightbringer has come to offer comfort to those who are suffering the misfortunes of war. Lord Lothar has entrusted to you the task of protecting Lightbringer and his entourage as they travel to the island township of Caer Darrow.

Objective: Escort Lightbringer to the Circle of Power at Caer Darrow.

Opening Maneuvers: Our Commander has decided to attempt a bold maneuver. Spies have reported that our land forces may not be able to deal with the heavily fortified Orcish settlement that separates us from Lightbringer, so we have endeavored to clear the seas of ships and trust Fate to deliver him safely to the Circle. Our first task was to assemble all our warships into a tight cluster; then we sent a single fast Destroyer south to draw out the enemy ships guarding the way to Caer Darrow. Once those had been eliminated, we decided not to risk doing the same with the traitorous Elven Destroyers beyond the gauntlet of Cannon Towers, for they are quite a bit smarter than Orcs and would perceive our trap. Instead, two more Horde destroyers were drawn out of the other passage to Uther and were sunk, leaving the sea lanes mostly open.

Carrying Out Our Orders: Our four Transports were then prepared for a dangerous mission. All unnecessary deck hands were invited to stay safely ashore with the troops. These four ships then set out unescorted toward Lightbringer. We sent our prayers after them, knowing that not all of them would return. As they sailed quickly through the Gauntlet, the Cannon Towers could not reload fast enough to hit them all; all four arrived, damaged but still seaworthy. Uther boarded the strongest of the four and prepared to sail back. His transport was placed in the middle in the hope that the lead and trailing ships would draw most of the cannon fire. The plan worked, Gods be praised, but two of the four sank below the waves.

Securing the Area: With Uther safely among the warships, our entire flotilla set out directly for Caer Darrow. With so many targets, the second Gauntlet could not possibly stop them all. Even the enemy Battleship near our goal was too busy with our warships to notice the Transports sneaking past. As soon as Uther's craft landed, he raced for the Circle of Power and stood with upraised hands. Boiling thunderheads soon filled the sky and unleashed bolts of lightning on the Elven craft, utterly destroying them. With the forces of Nature on our side, the remaining Horde forces quickly abandoned their cause and retreated. Fate had smiled on us yet again, and the seed of hope had firmly taken root.

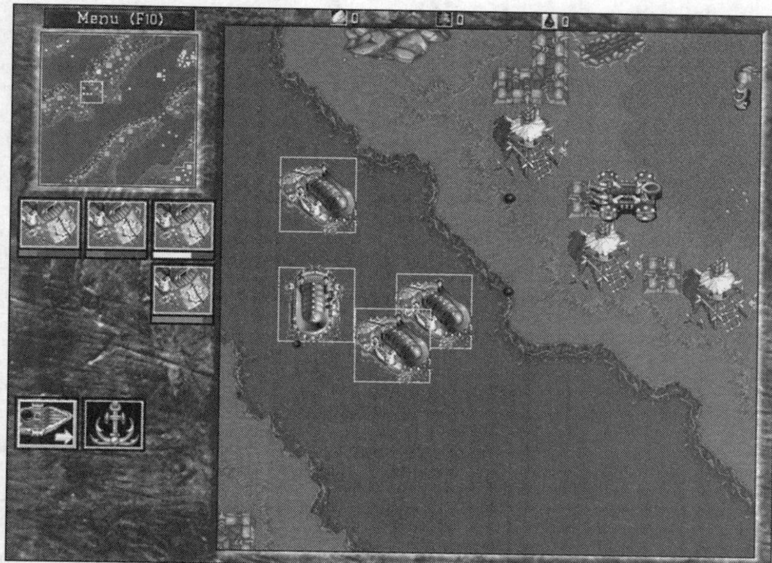

Towers can only fire at one target at a time.

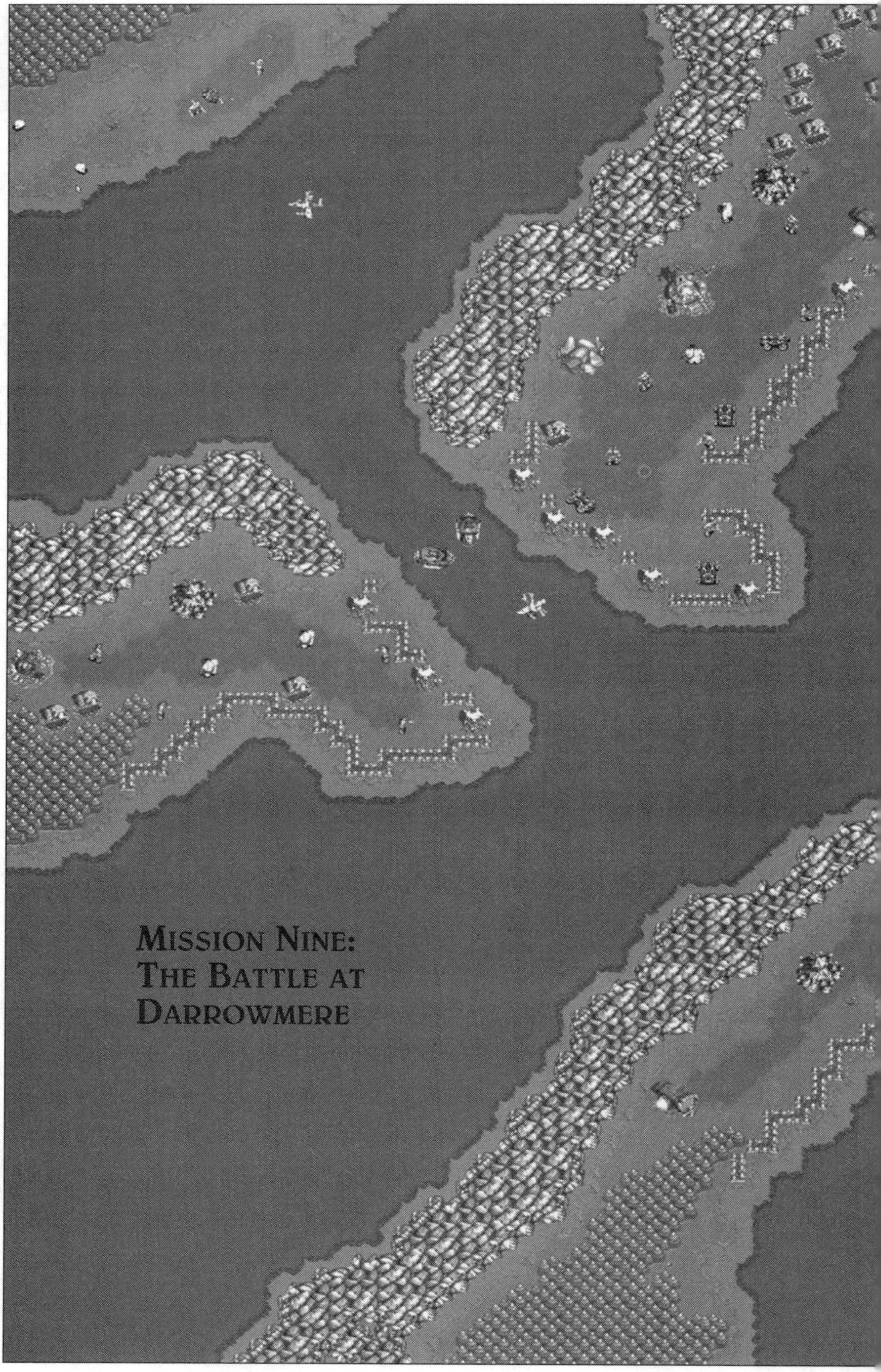

Mission Nine: The Battle at Darrowmere

Mission Ten: The Prisoners

Orders: After the battle at Caer Darrow, a number of Orcish soldiers were captured, along with the infamous Warlock Gul'dan. A crew of Alterac sailors were caught assisting the Horde during the battle and have been placed under close guard. Under the edict of Lord Lothar, you are to restrain the prisoners until they can be escorted to the capital of Lordaeron for interrogation.

Objective: Guard the enemy prisoners, construct transports, and escort at least four Alterac traitors to the Circle of Power at Stratholme.

Opening Maneuvers: Since we would need ships to carry out our orders, our first building priorities were a Lumber Mill, a Blacksmith, a Barracks, and, of course, a Shipyard. There was a plenitude of gold and lumber in the area, but we needed many workers to collect it. When the labor force had completed the Shipyard, we discovered that enemy Transports were unloading Orcs to the south of town. Although the few troops we had trained could deal with them for the time being, spies reported that they would soon arrive in increasing numbers. At the south edge of town we erected several Cannon Towers to deal with them, and fortified these with Farms and Archers for good measure. Once the town was reasonably secure, we concentrated on a Foundry for the production of Battleships.

Carrying Out Our Orders: Getting to the captured sailors was no easy task. A small Horde village separated the main body of water from the river snaking toward the prisoners, so we prepared an amphibious group of three Battleships and two Transports loaded with Footmen, Ballistas, and a couple of Peasants. First, we sent the Battleships in to take out the Tower and draw the Catapults closer to shore for their destruction. Once the coastline was clear, we moved our warships close to shore and landed the Transports. As soon as they unloaded, Ogres began pouring in from the settlement, but in their ignorance these monsters tried to concentrate on our Ballistas while Footmen and cannon fire cut them down. When the smoke had cleared somewhat, the Peasants built two Cannon Towers close to shore and the remaining Ogres were drawn in to their deaths. The rest of the village fell

quickly; the Ballistas made quick work of the enemy Juggernaught anchored on the river.

Securing the Area: In order to recover the prisoners, we first had to construct another Shipyard on the river. From here, we launched three more Battleships to deal with the numerous enemy Cannon Towers set up along the river, and only then did we launch a single Transport to pick up six of the captives. The rest were promised safe passage later, but at that time it was imperative that we get a few of them back to town. They were hurried from the river to the waiting flotilla on the sea, and were escorted back. We then forced four of them to stand on the mysterious Circle, which glowed brightly for a time, then faded. The prisoners simply stood dumbfounded until they were locked up in the Town Hall. Later, we received word that their memories had been thoroughly inspected from afar, and what had been found was not to our liking. The traitor nation of Alterac was to be destroyed for its crimes. I am deeply ashamed and angered that those of my own race would betray the Alliance. I shall not mourn their demise. . . .

Clear the riverbank with Battleships before sending a Transport.

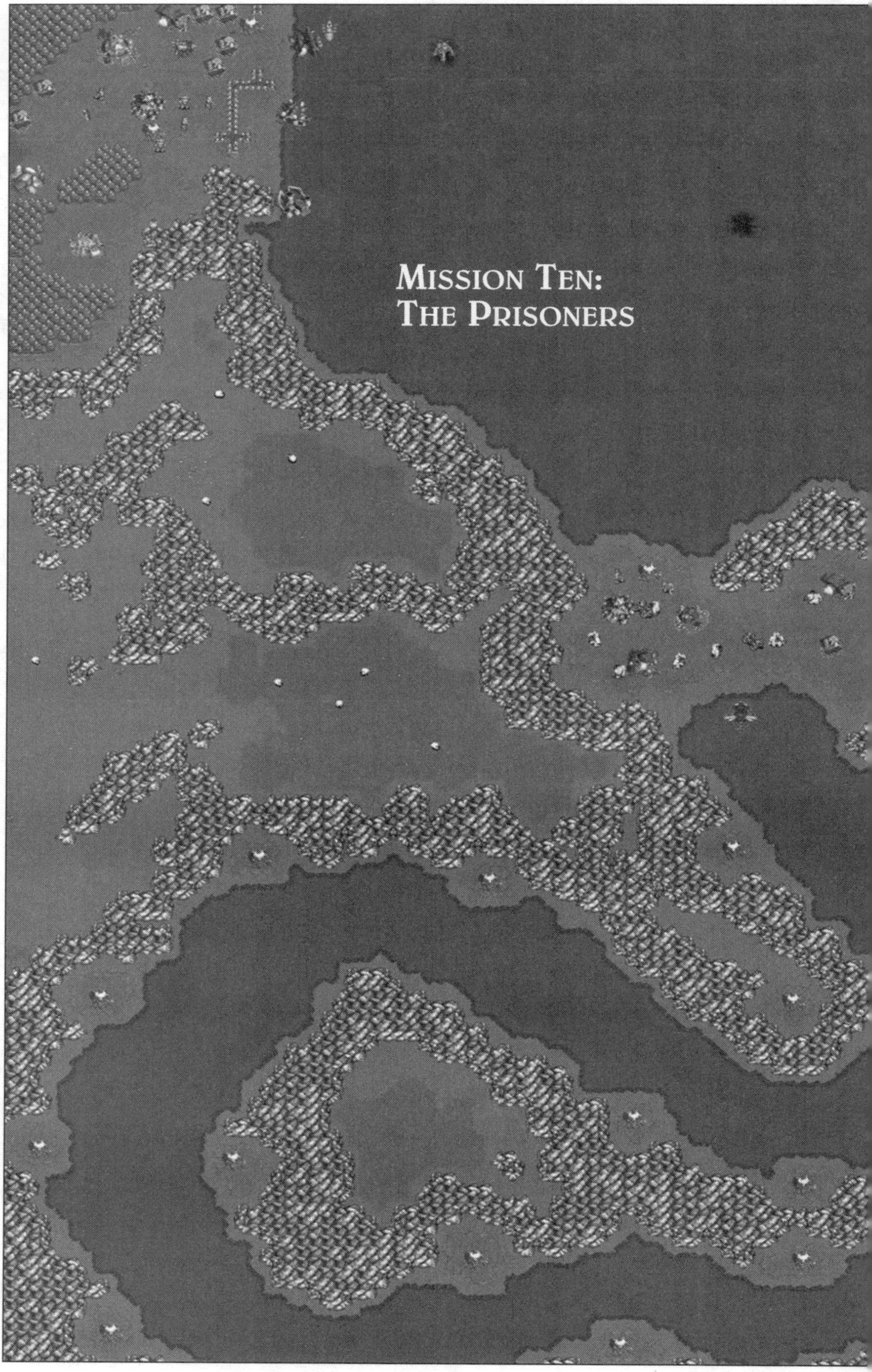

Mission Ten: The Prisoners

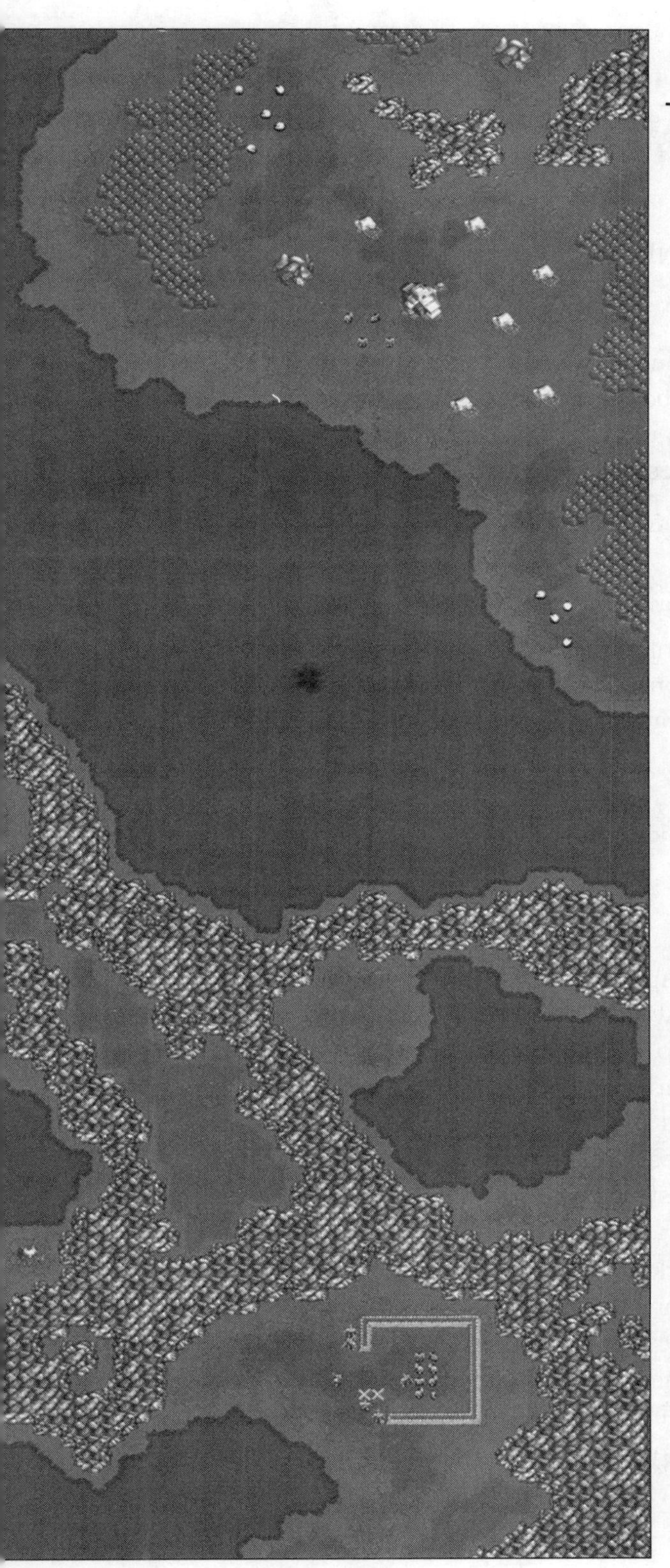

Mission Eleven: Betrayal and the Destruction of Alterac

Orders: Having interrogated the treacherous warriors of Alterac, Lord Lothar sends word that the Alliance has been betrayed. Lord Perenolde, sovereign ruler of Alterac, has been working with the Horde since the beginning of the war. It was Perenolde who provided the Orcs with the travel routes of the Elven strike force passing through Tarren Mill. The rebellion at Tyr's Hand was also started by Alterac spies in the hope of concealing the Orcish mining facility located there.

By decree of the High Command, the nation of Alterac has committed treason against the Alliance, and its union with the Orcish Hordes must therefore be broken. Lord Lothar has ordered that you free those persons unjustly held by Perenolde and enlist their aid in launching an attack against Alterac's capital.

Objective: Rescue the imprisoned Peasants and Mages from the camp in the northwest and return them to your base to launch a full-scale assault against the traitorous Alterac.

Opening Maneuvers: Rescuing the captive Mages and Peasants was of paramount importance, for we had no workers and no gold to train them. We formed a standard land attack group of Knights and Ballistas, then set out on the north road leading to the compound. Getting in was troublesome, but not difficult, since our Ballistas had a slightly greater range than the enemy towers. After breaking in and freeing the captives, we sent most of the force back to town, but not before destroying all we could.

Carrying Out Our Orders: With workers plundering the mines, we then began fortifying the town with Towers and Farms, closing off all the paths but one for our own troops to use. Next came the construction of Stables for our Knights, and soon after, the fortification of our Keep into a Castle. Since our attack plan required only Paladins and Ballistas, our final construction was a Church, and from then on, we concentrated on producing the necessary military units.

Time and gold were also spent on the Blacksmith, to provide the best possible weapons and armor. When we had gathered nine Paladins and four Ballistas in the courtyard, our force was deemed ready to make the assault.

Securing the Area: Moving out to the northeast, our Paladins led the way for the slower Ballistas, occasionally stopping to wait impatiently for them. At first we met with only a few enemies, but as we drew near the walls of the foul capital, greater numbers of Horde and traitorous Human forces slowed our progress considerably. After we had leveled several towers and secured an open area within the walls, reinforcements were called for and sent out while the Paladins practiced their healing arts on the wounded. Following the advice of our spies, we decided to march north along the inside of the west wall, taking out Towers along the way and ignoring lesser structures until later. Soon we were inside the heart of the capital, but we had taken a great deal of punishment. Still more Paladins were called for, and before long, we had our revenge on Lord Perenolde.

Bring Ballistas along to take out Towers from a safe distance.

Mission Eleven: Betrayal and the Destruction of Alterac

Act IV: The Return to Azeroth

Mission Twelve: The Battle at Crestfall

Orders: With the destruction of Alterac, the Orcish armies in the north have staged a massive retreat. Admiral Proudmoore sends word that Gnome Submarines have located the Horde's main naval base near Crestfall. Proudmoore believes that the Orcs plan to launch the remainder of their armada and retreat to the mainland of Azeroth. Lord Lothar has ordered you to destroy the base at Crestfall before the fleet can escape.

Objective: Destroy all Orc Transports, Oil Platforms, and Orc Shipyards.

Opening Maneuvers: Our first problem was feeding the large number of troops stationed inside the base, so the construction of two more Farms was urgently necessary. These we placed at the northern opening to impede enemy landing parties. Then our workers went to work in the mine; the resulting flow of income went for the training of even more Peasants. During this time, we gathered all our forces safely inside the base and brought our ships close to shore with a Flying Machine overhead to watch for enemy Giant Turtles. With this new threat in mind, we raised a Gnomish Inventor laboratory for the construction of more Fliers, and eventually our own submersible craft. Preparations for defense were completed with several Towers along the northern perimeter of town.

Carrying Out Our Orders: The next task was to collect oil for a naval force. Fliers reported a barren island far to the north with a dark patch on its east side, so we loaded up a Transport with two Ballistas and a Peasant in preparation for building on it. By that time we had another Flier in the air, which escorted the Transport and two Oil Tankers to the island, approaching it from the west side to avoid detection. After they had landed, a Tower was quickly raised on a small patch of flat ground that would allow Giant Turtles to be spotted and sunk by the Ballistas. On the north end of the island, a

Refinery was built at the same time as the Tankers constructed a Platform over the oil. When that task had been completed, a second Shipyard went up on the west side of the island and we began constructing Submarines at both.

Securing the Area: While waiting for the Submarines, our ships sailed out to the northeast, escorted by a Flier, to remove an enemy Oil Platform and stanch their flow of oil. This would help ensure that the sea remained clear after our Subs had had their fun sinking ships and Turtles. More Fliers were constructed as spotters for the Subs, and once their naval power had been reduced to flotsam, a Foundry was built for the construction of Battleships. These vessels were then fitted with the best cannons and armor we could make, and a flotilla of six sailed out to pound the enemy coastline. They were very careful to draw the Horde's Catapults to shore, where they were much easier to destroy. Next went the Towers guarding their shoreline structures, and finally the structures themselves.

Build a remote base near oil, and defend it well.

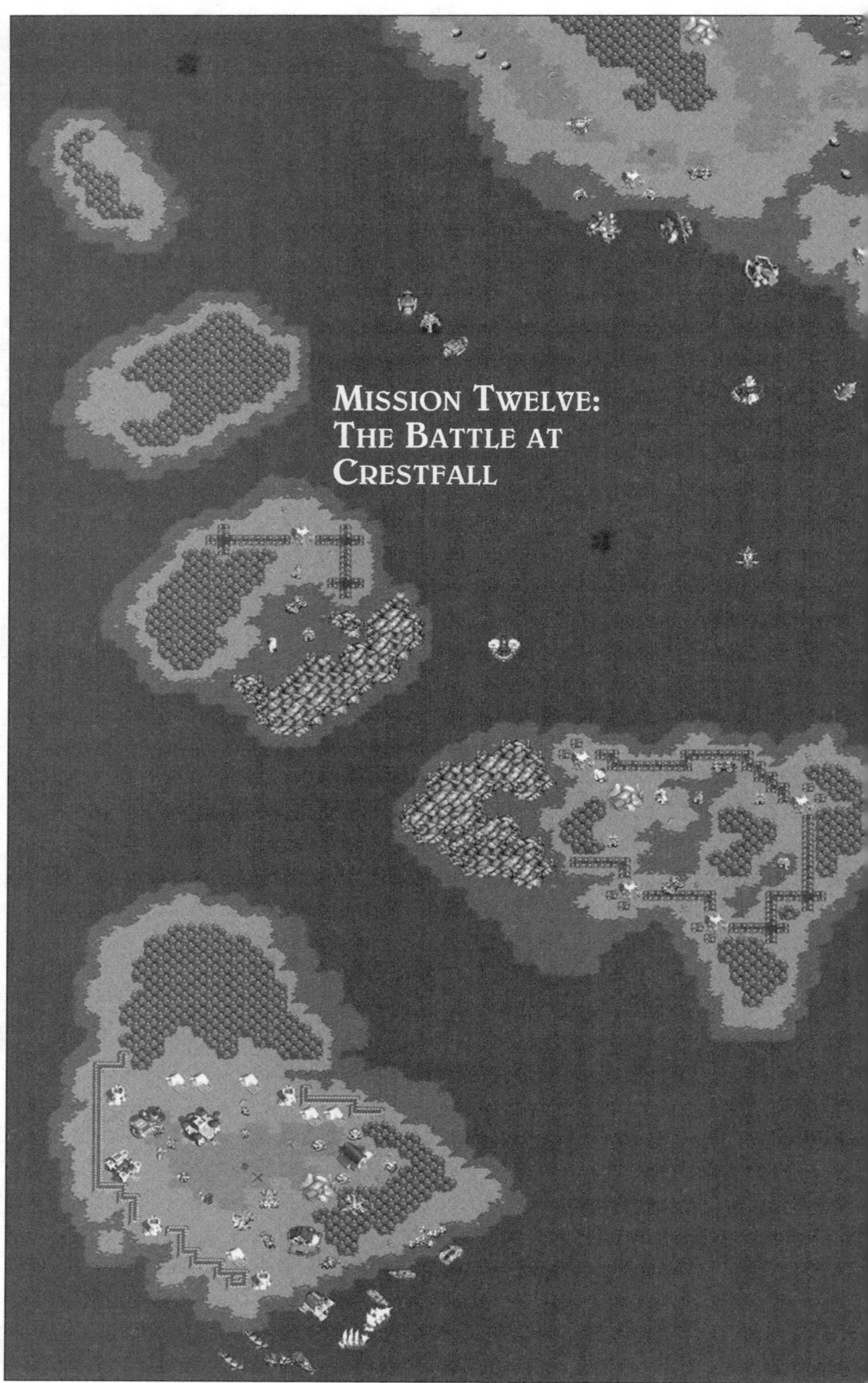

Mission Twelve: The Battle at Crestfall

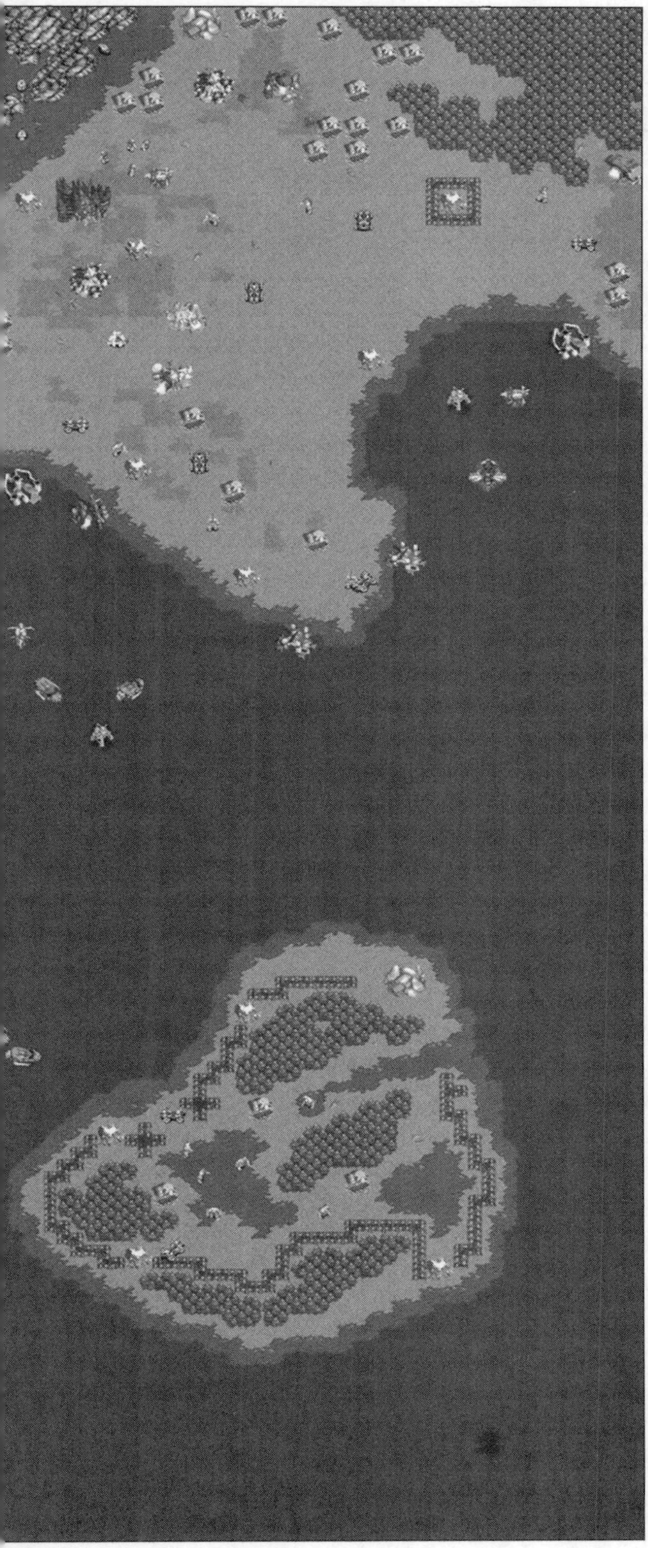

Mission Thirteen: Assault on Black Rock Spire

Orders: After the battle of Crestfall, the remnants of the routed Orcish fleet managed to reach the northern shores of Azeroth. Admiral Proudmoore believes that the Horde will attempt to reinforce their main Fortress at Black Rock Spire. Leading a large strike force of Lordaeron troops, Lord Lothar was sent to attempt a parley with the Orcish chieftain Orgrim Doomhammer. The war being all but finished, his intent was to accept the unconditional surrender of the Orcish Hordes. No word has been heard from Lothar or his strike force in days. . . .

Assuming the worst, Admiral Proudmoore and King Terenas agree that it falls to you to stage a final siege against Black Rock Spire. The feral Dwarves of the Northeron wildlands have offered the service of their Gryphon Riders to assist in the decimation of the foul Orcs that have desecrated their homeland and slain the leader of the Alliance forces.

Objective: Destroy Black Rock Spire and eradicate any and all enemy forces.

Opening Maneuvers: On our arrival, we found only workers and injured soldiers hiding in the few structures they had managed to defend. The town had been sacked once already, meaning Lord Lothar was likely dead already. When the survivors described the landing of enemy Transports, we decided to cripple their navy before concentrating on a major land assault. We immediately boarded our few warships and, escorted by a Gryphon, set out westward to follow the trail of the Transports.

Two enemy Destroyers were sunk before turning north, and near the mainland we spotted an Oil Platform being built. Not wanting to let them collect oil, we waited for the slower Battleship and planned an attack. Two enemy Juggernaughts waited to the southeast, while a Cannon Tower on land was judged able to strike targets only on the west side of the platform. First, we sent our Gryphon to chase and sink the Juggernaughts, while the warships sailed to the east side of the Platform to begin demolition. By the time the Gryphon had done its work, the Platform fell and was replaced with a Destroyer to prevent rebuilding. To complete the task, we then sent the Battleship and Gryphon north to sink the landed Transports, and thus prevented the Orcs under the orange standard from using them ever again.

Carrying Out Our Orders: Next on the list was the oil production of the red standard Orcs, and for this we sailed our Battleship eastward, followed closely by the remaining Destroyer and the Gryphon. We sailed directly into the harbor toward another newly built Platform, and again sent the Gryphon to remove a Catapult from the southeast shoreline near it. Then, while the ships pounded the Platform, our faithful Gryphon started on the landed Transports north of it to prevent them from making any deliveries. Next went the Cannon Tower west of the enemy Shipyard, and by then the Platform had been removed and replaced by a Destroyer. Waiting until the Tower was out of the way, the Battleship then went to work on the Shipyard, and its destruction ended their attacks by sea.

Securing the Area: A third and final threat to our base was the Dragon Roost on the central island, but this would require a bit more effort. While the Orcish navy was being neutralized, our workers built a few Guard Towers for minimal defense, then concentrated on all the structures and upgrades required to launch more Gryphons into the air. We also built a Foundry and a Refinery to produce more Battleships, but the mine was starting to run dry.

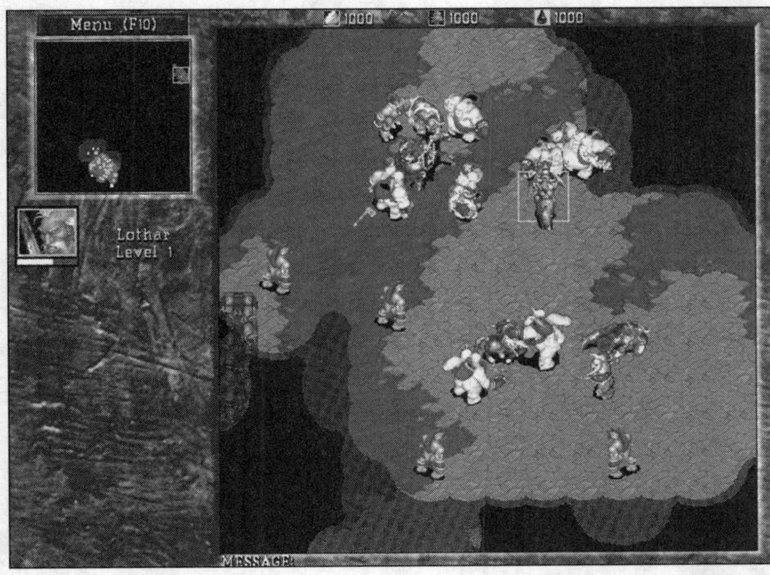

Sir Lothar betrayed!

Mission Thirteen: Assault on Black Rock Spire

To solve this problem temporarily, a single Transport was launched to ferry some workers east. There, the workers built a secondary Hall on a small island with another mine. This extra income allowed us to assemble a flotilla of four Battleships, four Destroyers, and three Transports with which to land a mixed force of Rangers and Knights on the central island.

First, the warships removed as many enemy Towers as possible, with the Destroyers concentrating on any Dragons that threatened. The land units came ashore on the north side and quickly swept into the village, slaughtering the defenders and finishing Towers before removing the rest of the foul structures. More workers were ferried in, and a third Hall was set up to plunder the rich mine there. From this point, the Horde was defenseless against the mobs of Gryphons we launched from four Aviaries. Standard landing parties of Knights and Ballistas made slow but steady work of anything remotely Orchish, while Gryphons circled overhead. Blackrock Spire was last to fall, and soon the Great Portal would receive the same treatment.

Mission Fourteen: The Great Portal

Orders: The Orcs have been driven from the Northlands as the hulking remains of Black Rock Spire lie silent among the freed lands of Azeroth. The battered remnants of the once-mighty Horde have rallied to protect their last bastion of hope—the Great Portal. With Lord Lothar dead, you have been given the duty of leading the forces of Lordaeron to ultimate victory over the Horde—a victory that proceeds from the destruction of the Great Portal itself. . . .

Objective: Destroy the Great Portal.

Opening Maneuvers: Before we could make the final assault on the Great Portal, we needed to find flat ground to build a village on. Predictably, there were strong defenses at the closest available land, so the first task was to clear the way for a landing with our few warships. Knights, Footmen, and Archers were loaded onto Transports and soon followed westward, for we would need to build quickly. A single Destroyer swept past the shoreline to the west to draw out the Catapults, then all three regrouped to attack single targets and retreat. This we repeated until all but one Tower remained on the shoreline; however, the Destroyers had been sunk, and the Battleship was taking on much water when we decided to make a landing. Knights and Footmen hit the north beach first and engaged the waiting Ogres, and as soon as there was room, the Archers came next to speed the slaughter with missile weapons. A few Knights were sent south to take out the Tower, and soon the area was secure enough to fetch the remaining units.

Carrying Out Our Orders: While building a Hall near the mine, our Archers were lined up to bring down marauding Dragons, and our two Mages stayed safely behind to launch Fireballs at the beasts as well. With this in mind, our next building priorities were Farms, a Barracks, and a Lumber Mill to train more Archers. These would ensure that Dragons were no longer a problem once we had a small army of them. The mine was quickly running out of resources, so we would soon need to claim another in the Ogre village close by to the north. To clear the way, our growing number of Archers were lined up behind Farms and better-armored soldiers, and a single Knight rode

forth to bring the Ogres into our arrow trap. Spies reported that three more Dragons far to the east were watching for smoke on the horizon, so we ordered our troops not to level the foul Orcish structures until we were fully prepared to greet them. A second Hall went up near the new mine to speed the collection of the great wealth within. This would ensure our survival against the next enemy village to the east, for soon we could afford to call on the skills of elite Elven Rangers to train our existing Archers in the ways of deadly accuracy. With these at our disposal, we began destroying the rest of the Horde structures and easily defeated the Dragons that came too late.

It was not long before we had two more Barracks, a Blacksmith, and a Stable to add more muscle to our forces. The muscle came in the form of many Knights and two Ballistas, all with the best weapons and armor we could make for them. Several Rangers and the Mages were left behind for defense, while a stalwart army marched eastward to begin clearing out the Orcs once more. We ordered them to stand their ground just outside in a standard formation of Knights first, Rangers behind, and Ballistas in the rear. Our greatest danger was the Death Knights that cast horrible plagues in our midst, so our forces were spread out to minimize their damage, and several Knights were kept moving to ride them down on sight. Once the defenders

The Great Portal will not be easily destroyed.

Mission Fourteen: The Great Portal

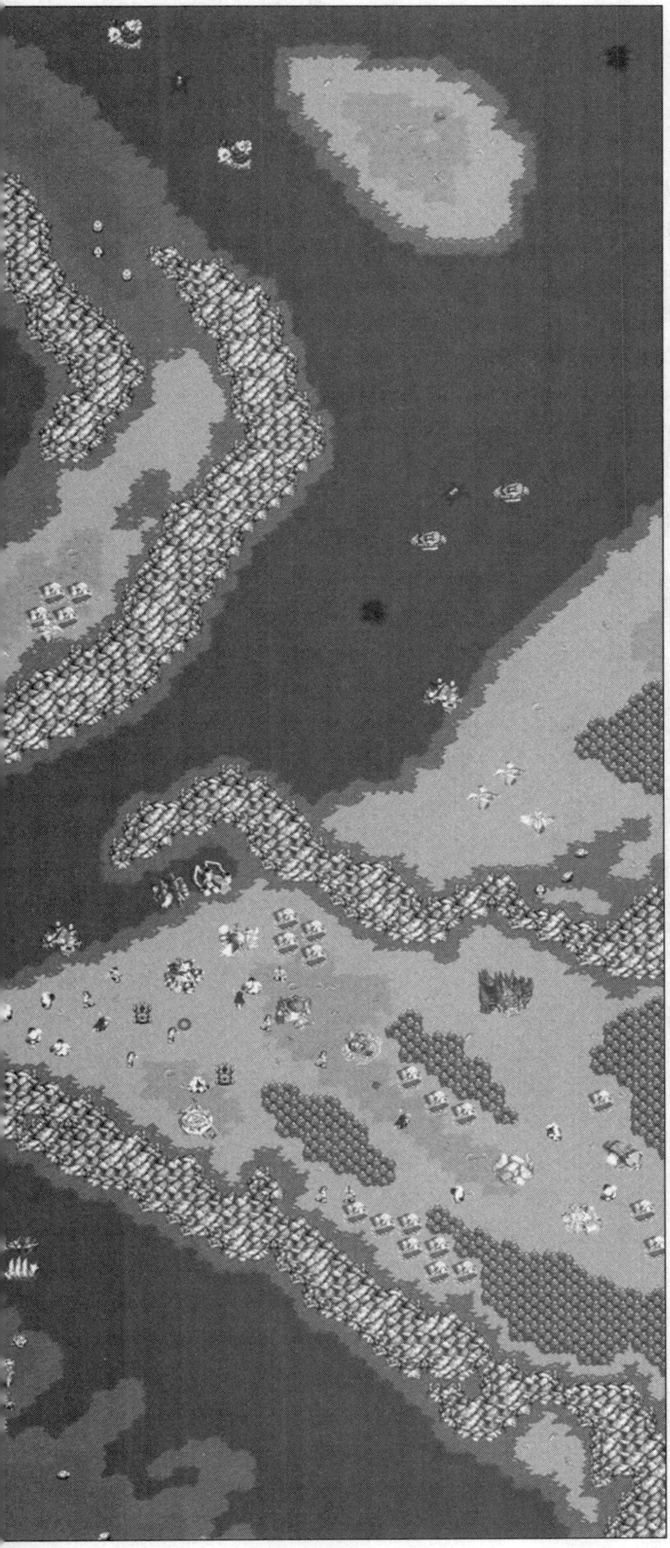

were mostly gone, demolition began once again while we hunted down any remaining enemies hiding nearby.

SECURING THE AREA: With a third mine and Hall to collect gold, we then built four Gryphon Aviaries to claim the skies for ourselves. Once we had a flight of eight in the air, these were sent out to wreak havoc on all the enemy ships in the waters surrounding the central island. In the meantime, a Gnomish Inventor supplied fearless Dwarves with explosives to bomb a path through the narrow line of mountains north of the third mine. This was done to place a Shipyard much closer to a supply of oil, and with the accompanying Foundry and Refinery, we could then produce Transports for the assault on the island. Our growing mob of Gryphon Riders then concentrated on drawing the defending Dragons and Demons away from their Guard Towers. Meanwhile, transports were loaded with Knights and Ballistas to do most of the demolition and slaughter on the island while the Gryphons kept the skies clear. Workers were brought to set up a second Shipyard on the inner ring of water, and by then the fate of the Orcish Horde was sealed. The glorious destruction of the Portal was followed with weeks of celebration worldwide.

METZEN·95

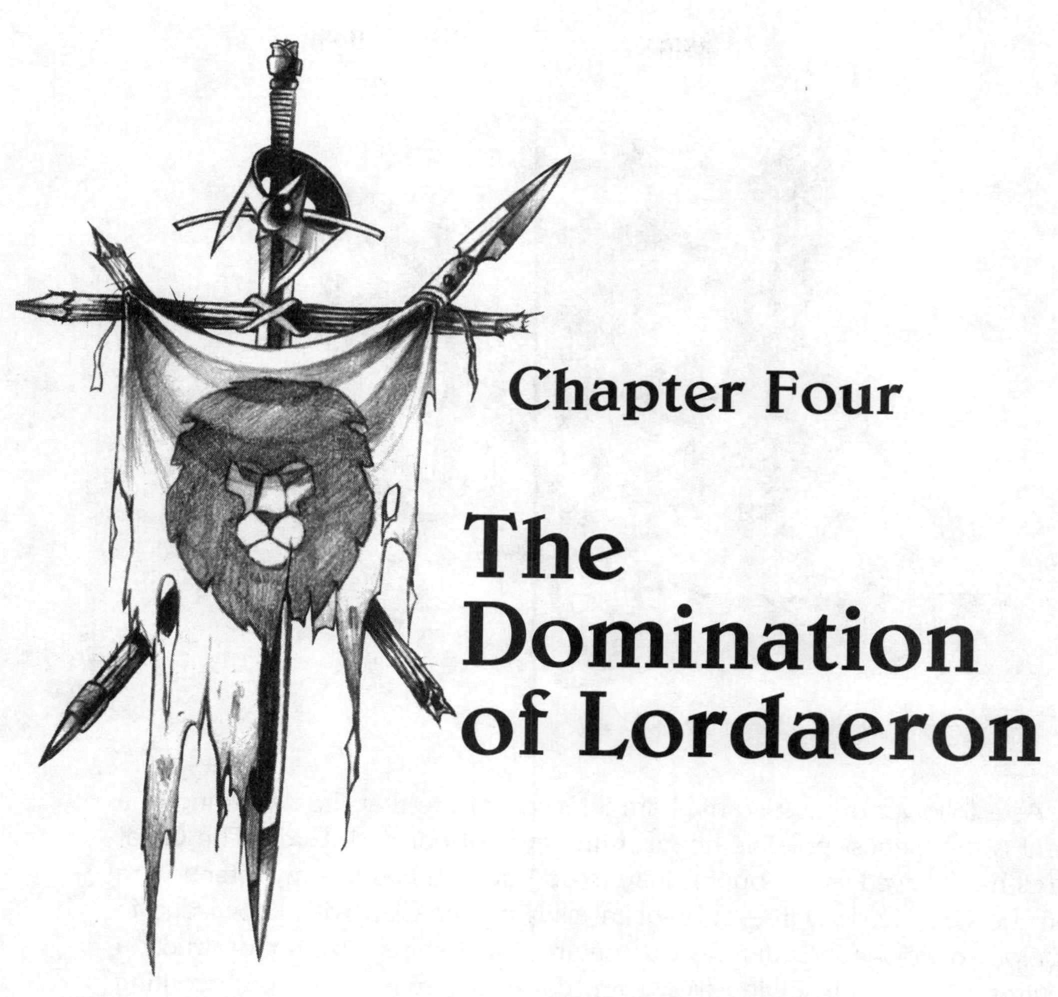

Chapter Four

The Domination of Lordaeron

I am Utok Scratcher, apprentice Shaman and chief advisor to a ruthless new commander of Clan Blackrock. I am called Scratcher for my habit of scribbling rather than mindlessly killing, but soon I shall be the one who laughs. For too long my people have ignored the need to record our methods. I am confident that these chronicles will benefit only those who recognize this need, mostly because there are very few of my kind who can read.

As a follower of mystic arts, I am intensely aware that the devouring of a world is the highest possible honor in the eyes of our dark Gods. The Great Portal has allowed us the opportunity to do just that, and it is my intention to arm the Orc, Troll, Ogre, and Goblin allies of our Clan with knowledge in addition to power; bloodlust is our nature, but the passion for destruction requires direction. Knowing this, I am compiling maps from our scouting reports, accompanied by descriptions of our orders and military tactics for clarification. These pages will be the weapon with which our Clan ascends above all others, to claim the honor of annihilating this new world and its inhabitants.

Act I: Seas of Blood

Mission One: Zul'dare

Orders: The Horde is preparing to launch an assault against the mainland of Lordaeron. Orgrim Doomhammer, War Chief of the Orcish Hordes and ruler of the Blackrock clan, has ordered you to establish a small outpost on Lordaeron's southern shores. To secure the Zul'dare region, as Doomhammer demands, you will need to construct a Barracks and several Farms to feed your troops. Your success may help us determine the extent of the pathetic Human defenses and the resistance they can offer against our forces.

Objective: Build four Farms and a Barracks.

Preparations for Battle: My commander has been given a pitiful number of troops and workers with whom to carry out our orders; yet we have managed to easily overtake a Human outpost and convert it to our cause.

Attack in groups to weigh the odds in your favor.

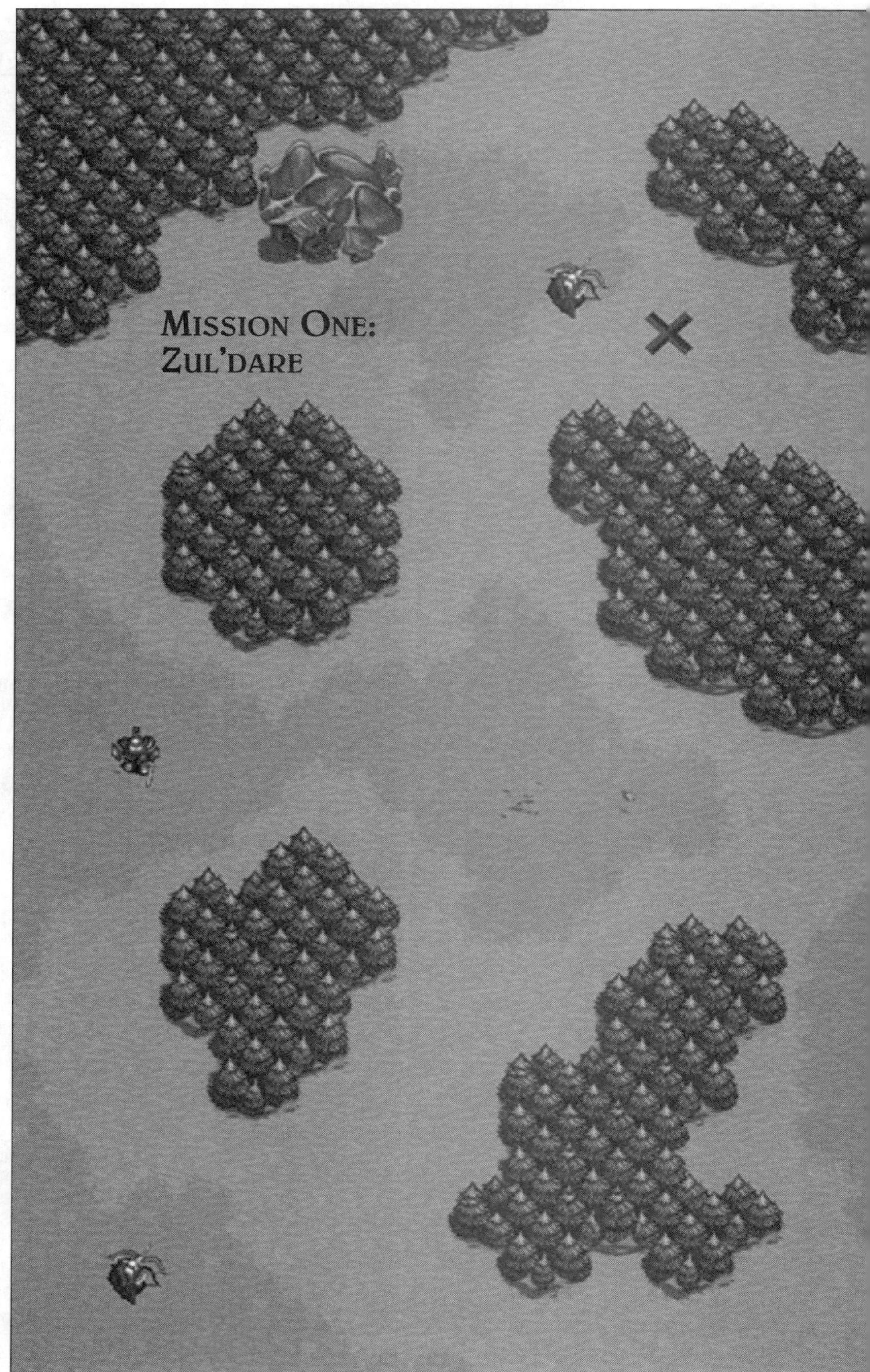
Mission One:
Zul'dare

Feeding ourselves after the long voyage across the Great Sea was necessary to keep our forces from killing each other over what little meat we had brought with us. Therefore, we beat an injured soldier into submission, made him a worker, and began fencing in new Pig Farms.

Methods of Destruction: Those who were not building were sent to labor in a nearby mine, for we would need mineral resources in addition to food. Bored with standing about, our troops banded together in a tight group and began patrolling the area; they managed to find a few scattered Humans to quench their thirst for blood. Only one of them returned, but by then we had begun construction of a new Barracks. This we would need for the coming reinforcements, so all available workers were whipped into helping.

Completion of Orders: With the Barracks completed, we needed only a bit more farmland to raise pigs, and soon the promised reinforcements arrived.

After a short time, all the Human spies in the area had provided skulls to adorn our Standard. With the area secure, we waited impatiently for new orders.

Mission Two: Raid at Hillsbrad

Orders: Our spies report that a band of Human soldiers have captured a war party led by Troll commander Zuljin and have taken them to the township of Hillsbrad. Seeing an opportunity to place these captives in debt to the Horde, Doomhammer sends you to ransom Zuljin and his Trolls. The War Chief believes that this raid on the unsuspecting settlement will strike terror into the hearts of those who would dare resist the Horde.

Objective: Rescue Zuljin and at least one other Troll, then return them to the Circle of Power.

Preparations for Battle: Our Grunts had gathered in the courtyard of the village; they were quite eager to seek carnage. In fact, every soldier in the vil-

lage marched north, shouting war cries, and left the Peons standing alone scratching their heads. The war party encountered feeble resistance and swept forward toward the enemy prison camp, leaving the village unattended. The workers would have the day off, it seemed.

METHODS OF DESTRUCTION: On reaching the camp, our troops first massacred the weaklings guarding it and patrolled about looking for more before venting their frustration on the walls.

COMPLETION OF ORDERS: Following the frozen river west and then south, a few more Humans were found and slaughtered—hardly worth the trouble—before we continued south to the abandoned village near Hillsbrad. This we claimed for ourselves.

Rescue allies behind enemy lines to add to your forces.

Mission Two: Raid at Hillsbrad

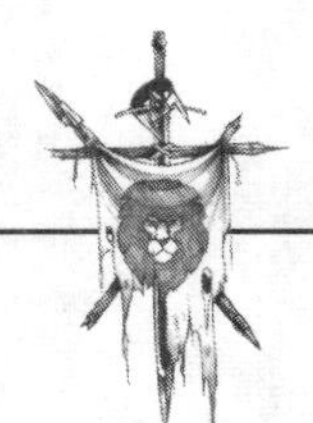

Mission Three: Southshore

Orders: In preparation for a final strike on Hillsbrad, the War Chief directs you to begin construction of facilities for the Orcish Armada near the Southshore region. Zuljin and his Trolls, eager to take revenge on the Humans who imprisoned them, have agreed to aid the Horde by supplying Axe Throwers and Destroyers to assist in the defense of your Southshore operation.

A Shipyard must be constructed for us to build our Wave Riders. You will need much of the black liquid known as oil to build your fleet. The seas are rich with this substance; your Oil Tankers will need to build Platforms where it is thick. The Tankers will bring this oil back to the mainland to power our ships of war. Our assault on Hillsbrad cannot begin until your task has been completed.

Objective: Construct four Oil Platforms.

Preparations for Battle: The training of more workers and the construction of Pig Farms came first to build up resources for a Lumber Mill. This we would need to process boards and masts for new ships, and to supply the materials needed for a Shipyard. Our soldiers practiced beating each other to relieve their boredom, for the cowardly Humans had yet to show themselves.

Methods of Destruction: Once construction of the Shipyard had commenced, we sent the Destroyer that had brought us to survey the rest of the island. It found several Human spies hiding in the tree line east of the camp, and easily blew them into tiny bits before returning to the Shipyards. We spotted several enemy ships and structures around a smaller island to the northeast, and with a growing number of workers and farms to feed our sailors, we soon launched our first Oil Tanker to build a Platform over a convenient patch of dark sludge nearby to the southwest. With this, we would also begin building more Destroyers to clear the way for more Platforms.

Completion of Orders: Four Tankers quickly provided the oil required to launch four more Destroyers; we sent these northward in a tight flotilla. The Humans were completely unprepared, having no spies left to report to them, and we laid waste to their work step-by-step. With five warships against no more than two enemy ships at a time, the task of clearing the seas was disappointingly easy. Our Tankers then moved in to replace the Human Platforms we had obliterated. Plans were made to conduct a final amphibious raid on Hillsbrad.

Pelt enemies on land with Destroyers.

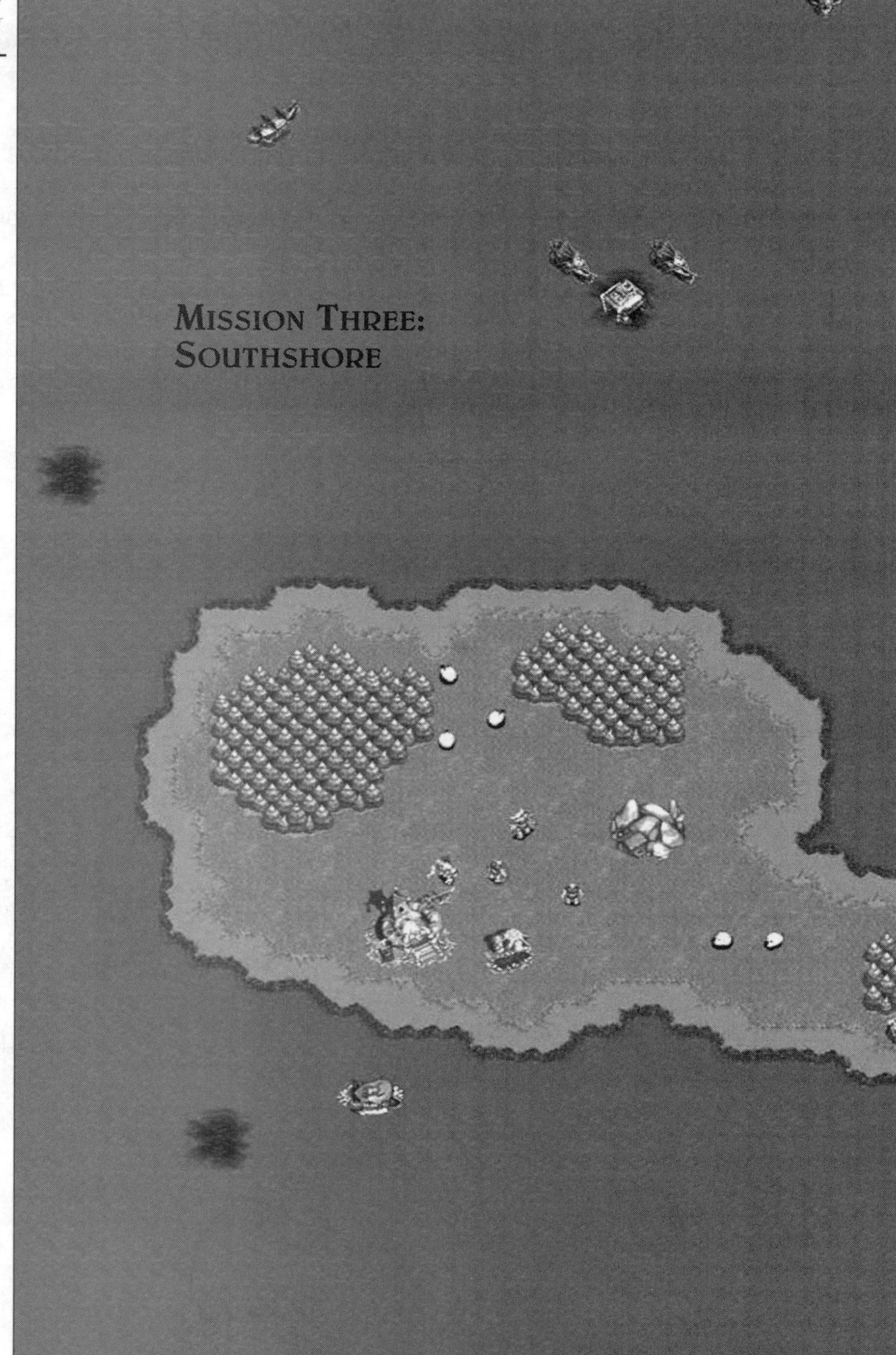

Mission Three: Southshore

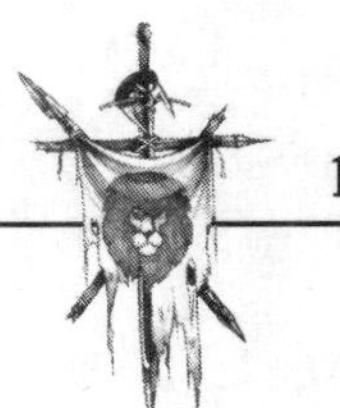

Mission Four: Assault on Hillsbrad

Orders: Now that the Armada is well supplied with the precious black substance that your Tankers have amassed, Doomhammer feels it is time to make a gruesome example of Hillsbrad. With the aid of new Refinery sites, you can build Transports to deliver your forces across the channel to the cowering Human settlement. All who oppose the Horde must be taught a harsh lesson! Leave no one alive!

Objective: Destroy Hillsbrad and all its defenders.

Preparations for Battle: We would need a large number of workers and farms to support this operation, and much time was spent making preparations and gathering resources before constructing the Lumber Mill and Shipyard required to begin the first stage. We kept the Destroyer that had brought us close to the shore north of town. With eight workers at our disposal, the Shipyard went up near where the Destroyer was anchored.

Methods of Destruction: Soon we had both a Shipyard and a Refinery on the north shore, with several Tankers gathering oil from a nearby patch. Four Destroyers were launched to clear the seas, then all five were sent far to the northeast where an enemy Platform needed removal. From there, we swept westward to the coastline near Hillsbrad, sinking a Transport that had managed to make a single delivery of Humans to our base. To prevent further annoyances of this sort, our warships made quick work of their coastal structures, leaving the nearby enemy Tower standing so they could watch. The destroyers remained near their shore; soon we would prepare to land our own force.

Completion of Orders: While a new Barracks provided training for six Grunts and six Trolls, we constructed two Transports for them and the Lumber Mill cut new, nicely balanced throwing axes for the raid. Once the Transports had been loaded and delivered to the waiting Destroyers, we

placed a single warship close enough to shore to pound their Tower. This panicked their soldiers into thinking they could stop us at the shoreline; as they came, our other warships opened fire. With the coast reasonably clear, the Transports landed and released our Hordes to level the town. All the defenders were slaughtered first; then their structures fell like straw huts. Soon word of our victory reached Doomhammer, who shortly thereafter rewarded us with an opportunity for more destruction near the mainland to the north.

Sink enemy Transports before they have a chance to make deliveries.

Mission Four: Assault on Hillsbrad

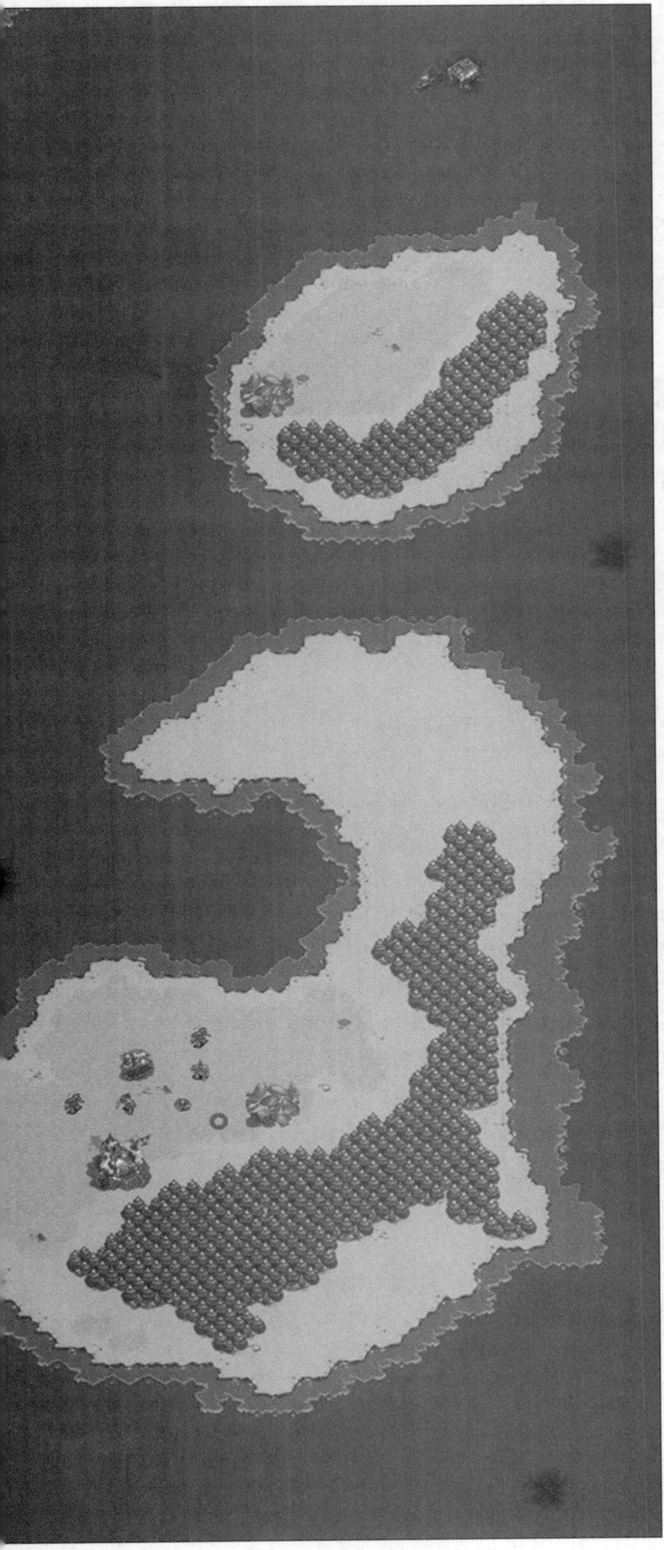

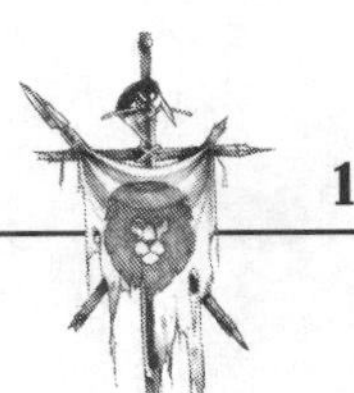

Act II: Khaz Modan

Mission Five: Tol Barad

Orders: The township of Hillsbrad has been decimated, and throughout the Human kingdoms the rumors of impending doom spread like wildfire. War Chief Doomhammer is pleased with your success and has deemed you worthy of a more difficult task. Troubles have arisen in the Dwarven lands of Khaz Modan. A task force of Stromgarde warriors has laid siege to Dun Modr, a vital staging area for Horde troops. You are to retake Dun Modr and then bring your forces to bear against Stromgarde's nearby island citadel of Tol Barad.

Objective: Retake Dun Modr and assault the citadel of Tol Barad.

Preparations for Battle: After unloading our forces, the Destroyers immediately sailed south to look for enemy Oil Platforms to seriously reduce their naval power while we established a base south of the landing point. All our troops swept into the village of Dun Modr and slaughtered the inhabitants before we brought in the Catapult to work on their structures. Once the village was secure, we summoned the workers and had them build two Farms north of the mine in a clearing, which would serve to block enemies from entering from that direction. While lumber was gathered to the east, a Great Hall was constructed as close as possible northeast of the mine, and more Farms were constructed in a defensive east-west line just south of the mine. During this time, we trained as many slaves as possible to work, for we would need to build up quickly.

Methods of Destruction: Our amphibious force would need many structures to produce the necessary warships and troops, so a Lumber Mill, a Blacksmith, and a Barracks headed the list. With these completed, a Shipyard was built on the east shore near an oil patch, and Tankers were

launched to exploit it. Our starting Destroyers had managed to prevent enemy Tankers from installing another Platform by resting on the oil, which prevented them from producing more ships, so we had little to worry about. Soon, we had a flotilla of six Destroyers and two Transports with which to make the assault.

Completion of Orders: We loaded eight Grunts and four Catapults onto the Transports and set out for the west side of the enemy city, behind the mine there. It was only a matter of time before the town was in ruins. The Destroyers went out to clear the seas of any remaining enemy ships. Our Gods were pleased that day; our ascension to power was well under way.

Catapults make quick work of structures, but are vulnerable to mobile enemies.

Mission Five: Tol Barad

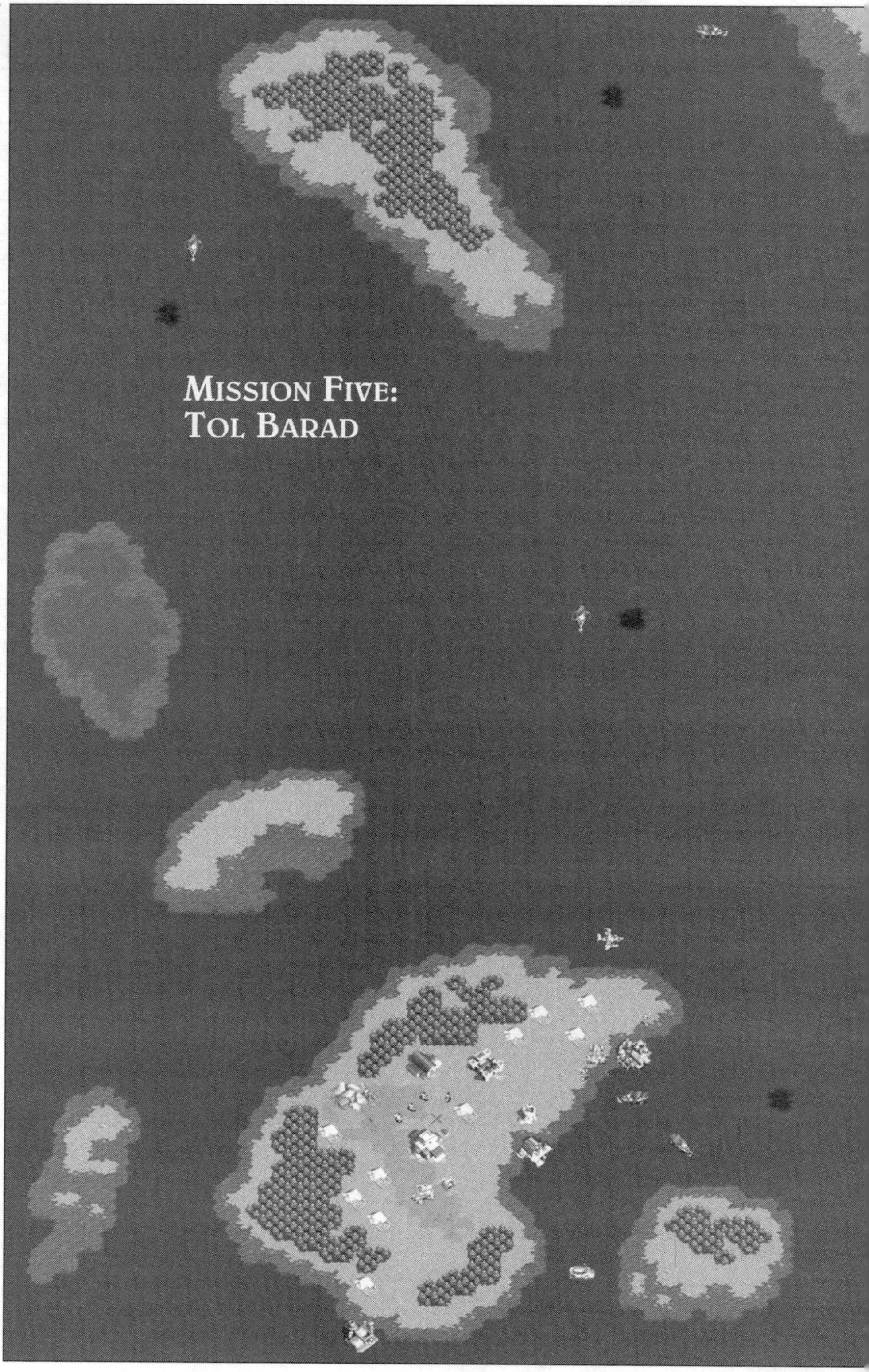

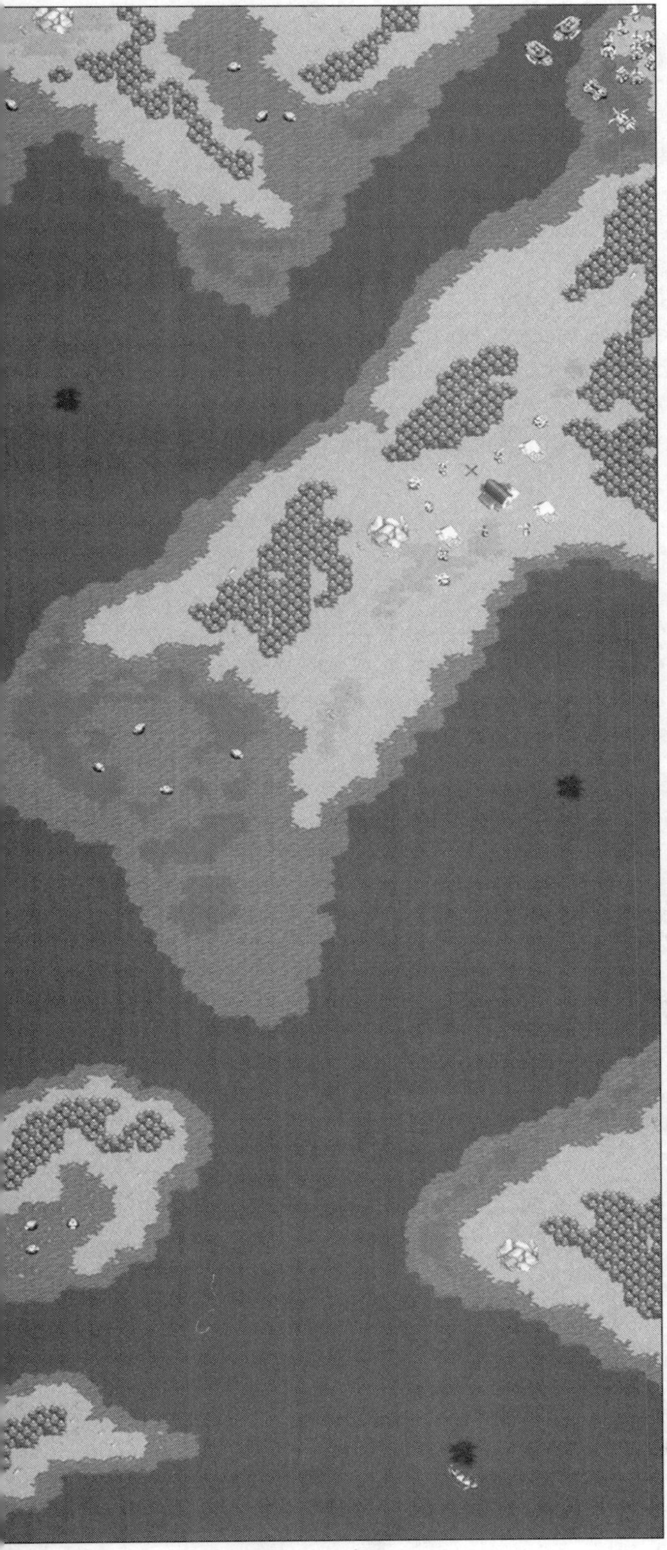

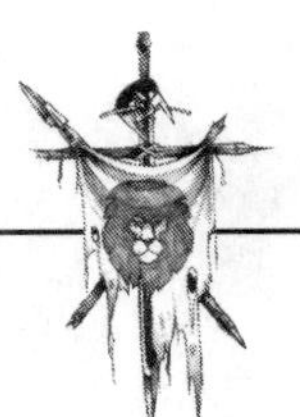

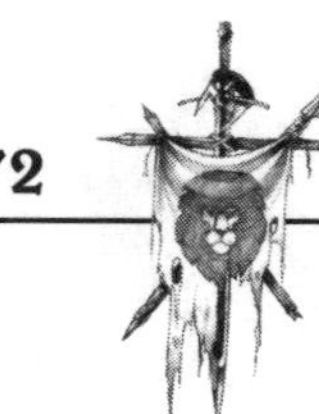

Mission Six: The Badlands

Orders: Doomhammer has sent word that the Ogre-Mage Cho'gall, chieftain of the Twilight's Hammer clan, is personally inspecting the Refinery at Grim Batol. Cho'gall and his convoy will be traveling through the badlands of Khaz Modan; an ambush by Stromgarde warriors is expected. The War Chief expects you to escort Cho'gall and his minions through this region. Should he die, your life will be forfeit as well. . . .

Objective: Escort Cho'gall to the borders of Grim Batol.

Preparations for Battle: The importance of this mission earned us the use of a powerful army, which we assembled before setting out southward along the coastline. Cho'gall and the Catapults remained in the rear; the other troops led the way for them. Occasionally Cho'gall would create floating Eyes to inspect ahead of us. Soon, we came to the first Human defensive wall.

METHODS OF DESTRUCTION: The Catapults were brought to the front and trained on the enemy Ballista behind the wall. With that threat removed, the troops set about knocking down a section of wall to slaughter the other defenders. We were constantly ordering them to return to the main group, for their bloodlust kept leading them inland to alarm more enemies. Continuing south along the coast, we encountered a second group of enemies with Destroyers close by, so we gutted the Humans before sinking the ships with our Catapults.

COMPLETION OF ORDERS: With our goal in view to the east, we ripped apart a final large group of Humans before we marched in and claimed the village for ourselves. It was almost too easy. After Cho'gall had made contact with higher powers on the Circle, our bloodthirsty and frustrated troops were released to wreak havoc wherever they wished. Many did not return, but Orcs will be Orcs.

The Eye of Kilrogg safely reveals hidden dangers.

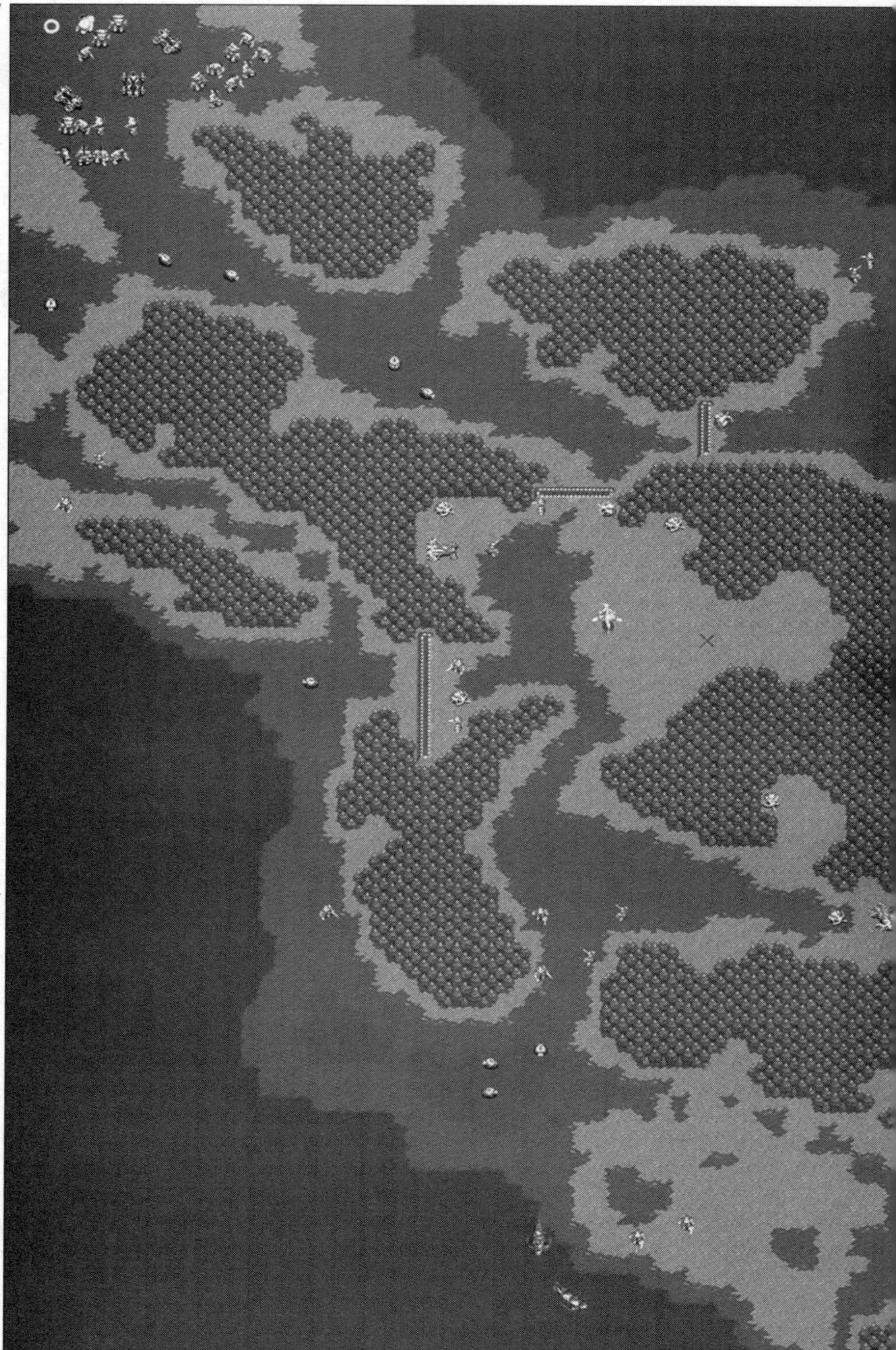

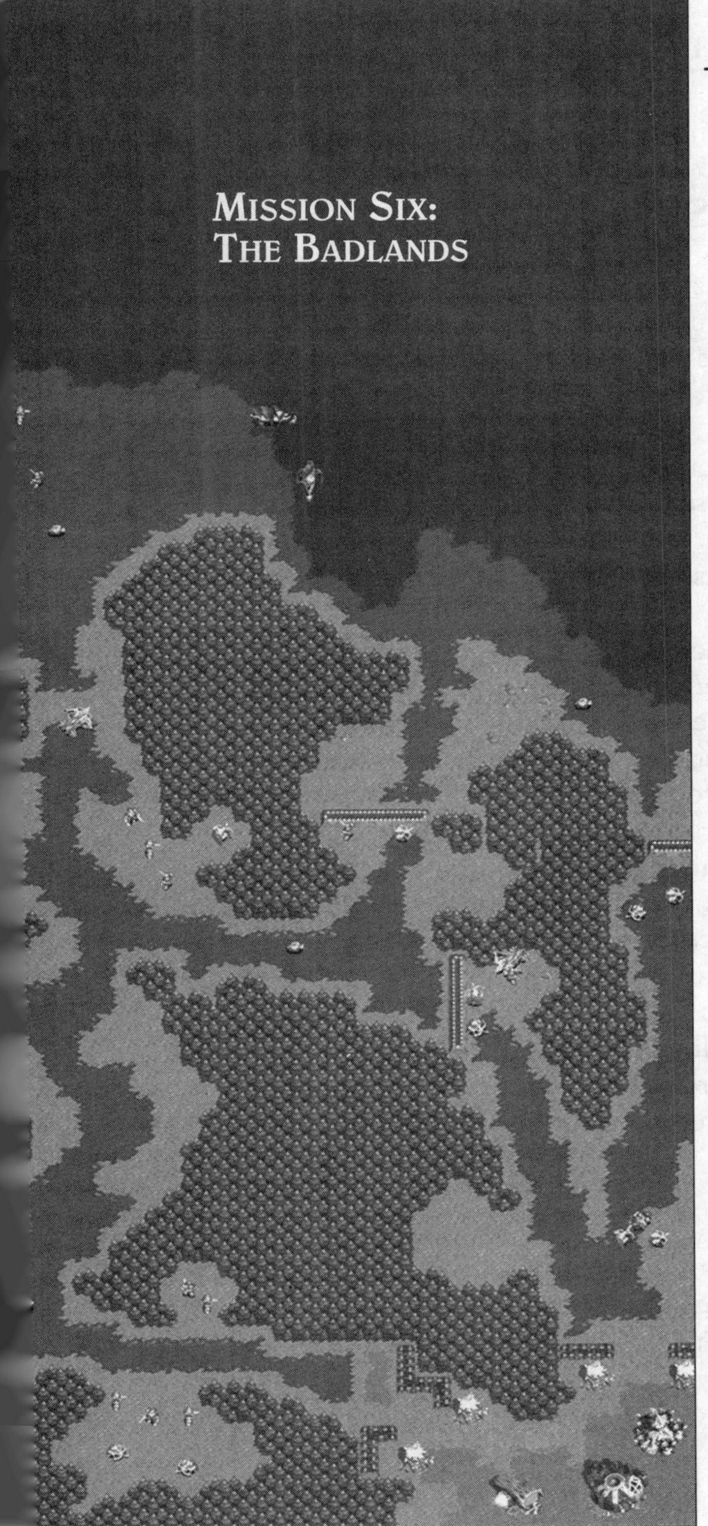

Mission Six: The Badlands

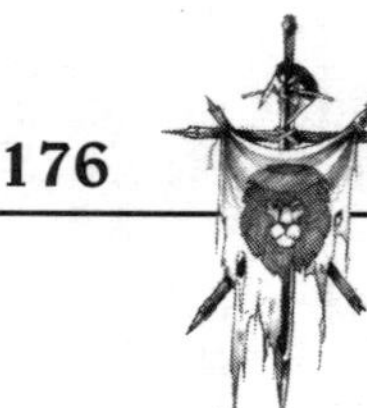

Mission Seven: The Fall of Stromgarde

Orders: Cho'gall reports that the Khaz Modan Refineries are well maintained and fulfilling their quotas. The Horde will now have more than enough oil to mount a fierce campaign in the lands far to the north. Only the troublesome Human defenders of Stromgarde remain to be dealt with before sending the Horde on its next journey.

The Human fleet has captured a group of our Transports just south of Stromgarde's capital. Recapture these vessels and then lay waste their capital.

Objective: Recapture the Orc Transports and destroy Stromgarde.

Preparations for Battle: First we called in the Destroyers from the west, gathering them together before concentrating on the two approaching enemy Destroyers. With all four intact, they sailed into the harbor and quickly boarded the Transports, reclaiming them. The inland troops then marched north, leaving the workers behind, and fought a path to the waiting Transports while the Destroyers lingered near shore for cannon support. With all units safely aboard, the flotilla sailed north and landed on the east side of a large island, killing the defenders there and bringing down a Tower that guarded a mine. The Destroyers continued north and west around the tip of the island, heading for an enemy Oil Platform to destroy it.

Enemy Destroyers attempted to stop us, but our tight formation eliminated them one at a time with combined fire. The Platform was removed and a Destroyer sat directly on the oil to prevent construction of a new one. Their naval power was crippled, leaving us plenty of time to build up safely on the island.

Methods of Destruction: While we were removing the wall around the mine entirely to make room for the workers, a Great Hall went up as close as possible to it. Then we began cutting lumber on the south side of the western forest. Farms were next for the training of more slaves, and a Lumber Mill was constructed near the forest with all available workers helping. With a growing force of laborers, soon we also had a Blacksmith and a Bar-

racks in operation. To fortify our base, Farms were constructed on the north side, with Cannon Towers behind them to fend off occasional raids. Next, we fortified the Hall with stone and iron, then built a Shipyard on the east shore near some oil. Preparations for our invasion continued with an Ogre Mound; then a Foundry and a Refinery allowed construction of more ships. With all necessary structures in place, we spent extra time and gold to upgrade our weapons and armor for soldier and ship alike and gathered our forces to make the assault.

COMPLETION OF ORDERS: A flotilla of four Destroyers and two Transports sailed out, carrying seven Ogres, four Catapults, and a Peon. The Destroyers cleared the way for a landing on the west side of the enemy; the worker set up a makeshift Barracks on enemy soil while the army stood guard. When the attack commenced, the Catapults removed defensive structures from a distance; the troops were constantly ordered to stay near them. Slowly we leveled the city from west to east, replacing fallen Ogres as

Make a run for your Transports to avoid fighting.

Mission Seven: The Fall of Stromgarde

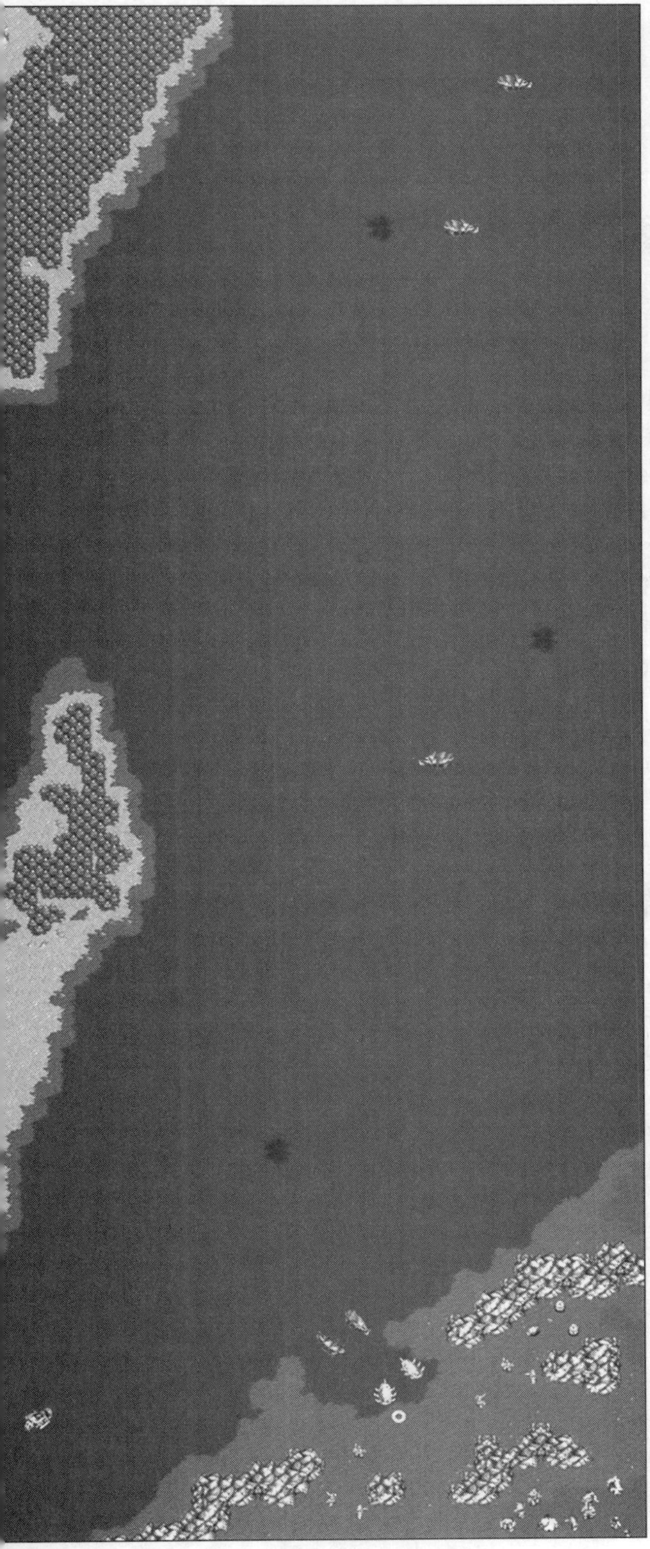

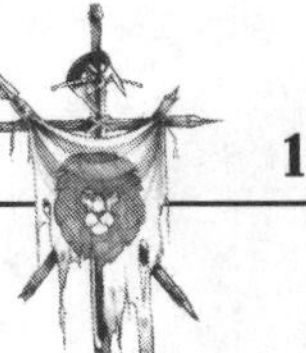

necessary. Their Shipyards fell last to the Catapults, as well as their ships anchored in the harbor. Had we not placed a Barracks on the island, it would have been much harder to ferry replacements in. The invasion was deemed a major success. Fear and honor were heaped on the name of our commander. The tide of war was slowly turning in our favor.

Act III: Quel'thalas

Mission Eight: The Runestone at Caer Darrow

Orders: Your forces have been assigned to an area along the southern border of the Elven kingdom of Quel'thalas. Gul'dan, hoping to sow the seeds of chaos among the Human and Elven allies, has located a mysterious Elven artifact near the Keep of Caer Darrow. This huge, monolithic Runestone is guarded by a Human Castle on the small island located in the middle of Darrowmere Lake. You must destroy the forces that guard this relic and gain control of the Runestone for the use of the Horde.

Objective: Destroy the Human Castle and secure the Runestone.

Preparations for Battle: Since many of the necessary structures were already in place, our first task was the collection of resources for the invasion. Farms and slaves were created at a dizzying pace; Tankers set out southward to install a Platform and collect oil. Our warships stayed close to shore with a Zeppelin overhead; our Stronghold and Towers were upgraded as soon as our supply of resources permitted. Construction continued with a Foundry, a Refinery, and a Goblin Alchemist to produce more Fliers for the invasion. A second Shipyard was erected to double our Juggernaught production, and soon we had a powerful flotilla in the bay.

Methods of Destruction: Six massive Juggernaughts sailed out with a Zeppelin overhead to spot enemy submersibles, and we began the slow process of pounding the defenses on the central island. Keeping the ship together, we made constant strikes on single targets, then sailed back out of range to regroup. Enemy Ballistas were drawn out to shore for their destruction. With most of the Towers removed, we started on their Shipyards at both villages. Many of our Juggernaughts were sunk in the process, but more

were constantly produced to replace them. Once their naval power was decimated, the Juggers moved in close to shore on the island and removed most of the land structures to make way for a landing.

COMPLETION OF ORDERS: While the island was being pounded, an Ogre Mound went up within our base and twelve Ogres were loaded on Transports to assault the island. Resistance was minimal and soon the Runestone was ours. This sent a clear signal to the remaining Humans in the other village, who beat a hasty retreat. Our might was growing daily and our morale was higher than it had ever been, even during the destruction of Azeroth.

Danger lurks below the waves.

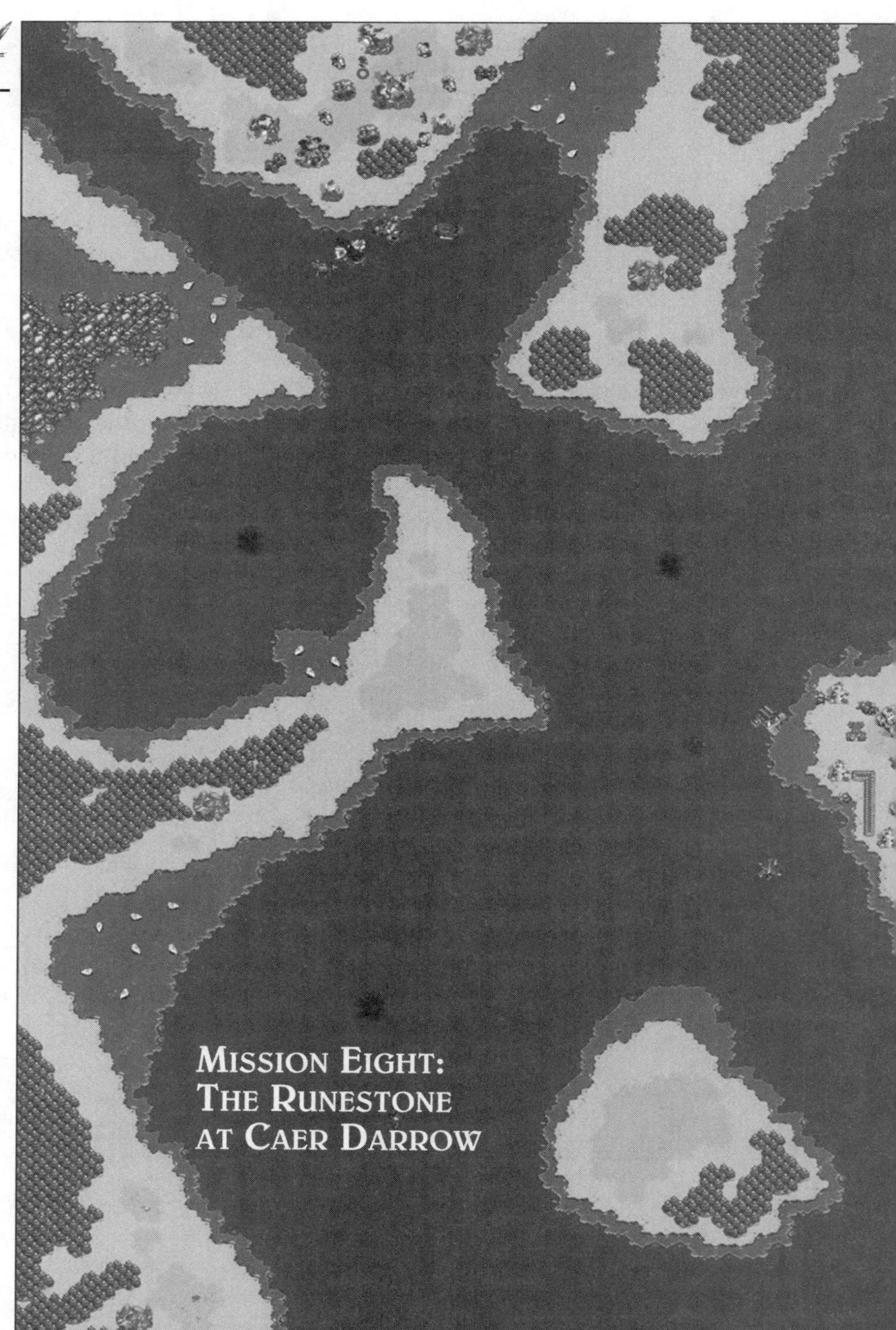

Mission Eight: The Runestone at Caer Darrow

Mission Nine: The Razing of Tyr's Hand

Orders: With the capture of the Elven Runestone, Gul'dan has been able to warp the power it contains to mutate an entire legion of his loyal and ruthless Ogres into wielders of arcane magicks. Along with this transformation, these Ogre-Magi have been granted deadly magicks and a malicious cunning rivaling that of Gul'dan himself. You are to employ the Ogre-Magi in the creation and defense of a Fortress at the mouth of Tyr's Bay, cutting off the Human supply lines into Quel'thalas.

Objective: Construct a Fortress and a Shipyard on the island at the mouth of Tyr's Bay.

Preparations for Battle: As usual, we needed scores of slaves to build and collect material, so training began in earnest while our warships sailed out with a Flier to quickly eliminate an enemy Platform to the northeast. This cut their oil production in half. Our own oil production started with the launching of a Tanker. A Foundry went up next to produce Juggernaughts. Towers were erected to guard the coastline against submersibles and landing raiders. A large labor force was amassing wealth to build the necessary warships.

While the bay filled with our ships, we upgraded our Hall into a Stronghold, built an Ogre Mound, and then provided an Alchemist lab for more Zeppelins.

Methods of Destruction: Once we had six or seven Juggers at our disposal, we sent them out with Fliers and began pounding the coastline, concentrating on the enemy Shipyards to put an end to their naval force. During this time, we again fortified our Stronghold into a stalwart Fortress; we also erected an Altar of Storms to instruct our Ogres in the dark arts. A constant stream of Juggers sailed out to replace those we had lost. A second Barracks went up to double the training of Ogre-Magi.

Completion of Orders: After the enemy Shipyards had been removed, we began assembling an amphibious force of two Transports loaded with three Catapults, eight Ogre-Magi, and a single worker. Our Juggers then

began carefully taking out Towers and Ballistas on the central island while avoiding those on the mainland. When the Transports arrived and landed, supported by cannon fire from nearby Juggers, the Ogres quickly cast Bloodlust on themselves and set to work demolishing the remaining forces on the island, staying near the Catapults until they could remove the rest of the Towers from a safe distance. All that remained was to build the necessary Fortress and Shipyard on the island, sealing the fate of the Alliance forces on the mainland.

Overzealous Juggernaughts are easily sunk by Cannon Towers.

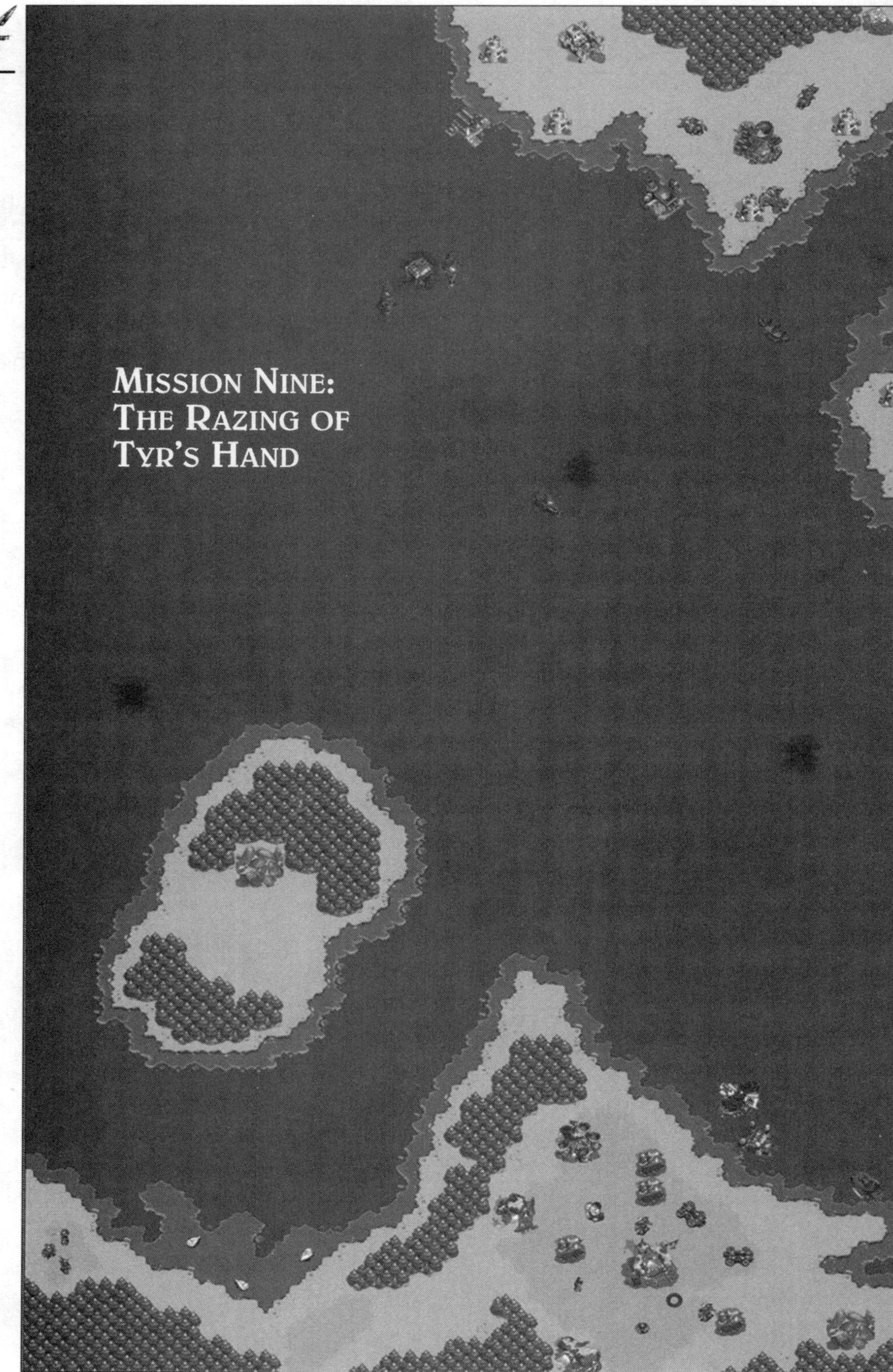

Mission Nine: The Razing of Tyr's Hand

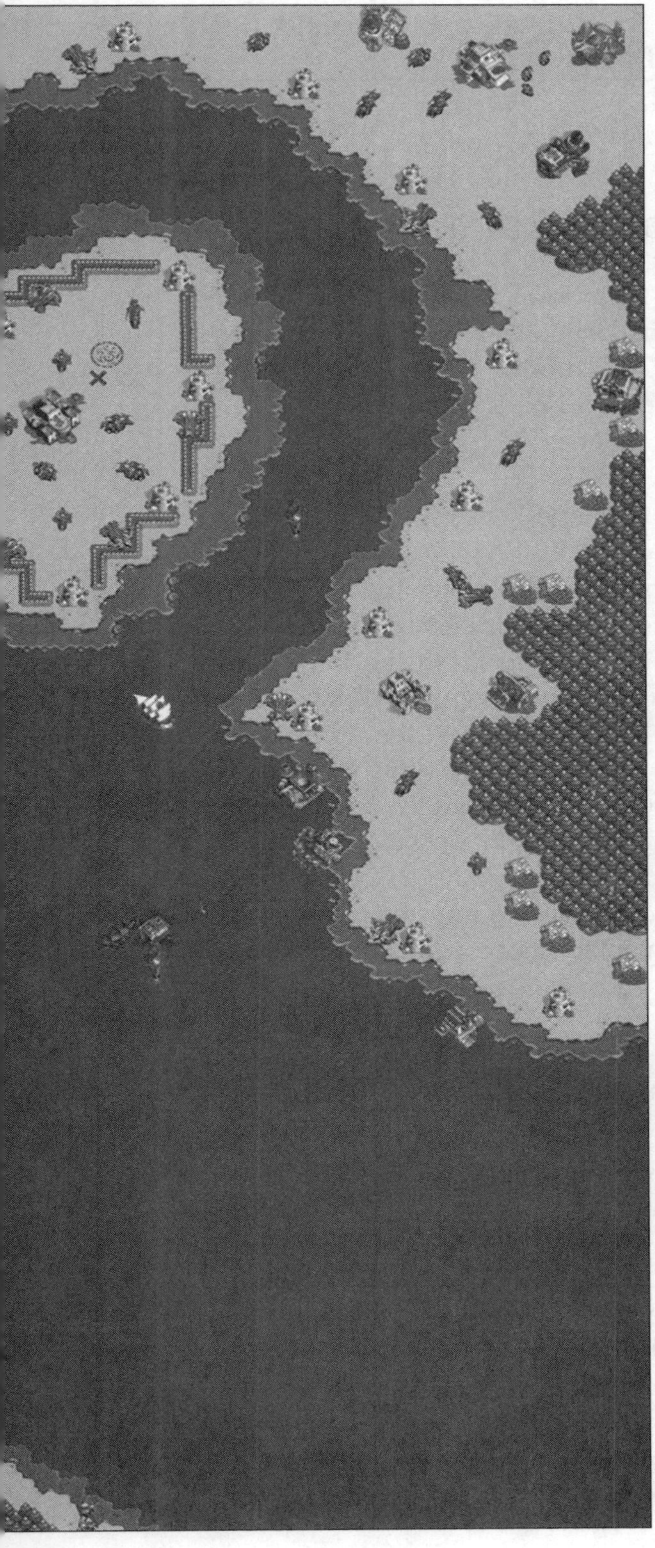

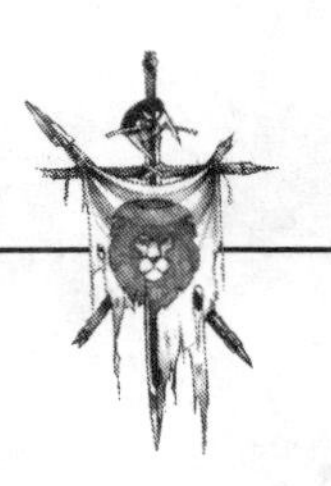

Mission Ten: The Destruction of Stratholme

Orders: Stratholme, the chief source of Alliance oil in the north, is preparing to deliver massive amounts of oil to the kingdoms in western Lordaeron. You must sabotage their Refineries and Oil Platforms to halt this shipment. Once Stratholme's ability to gather and process oil is removed, proceed to crush any and all resistance offered by the Alliance.

Objective: Destroy all Oil Platforms and Refineries; destroy Stratholme.

Preparations for Battle: First our Sappers had to blow a path inland for our troops; this provided an impressive display of their talents. Our plan was to take the city by land first, then to build ships to finish the job, so our forces prepared to march further north after slaughtering the Alliance forces to the east. One of our slaves remained to build a Hall to the north of the gold mine nearby; the rest headed out to set up closer to the enemy city. Again we gutted any enemies we encountered, but avoided the large clearing at the city entrance, not wishing to draw their attention before we could build. We built a second Hall as close to the other mine as possible, and quickly built Farms for food and defense to the west to impede enemy forces coming from that direction. With supplementary income from the southern mine and more workers from both Halls, resources piled up quickly and we could build as fast as possible.

Methods of Destruction: We had to erect several structures before building up for the land assault. First was a Barracks to start the training of Grunts, for we would need all the forces we could muster to defend the settlement. A Lumber Mill and a Blacksmith went up next, then a second Barracks to double our troop production. We were careful not to cut lumber near the Hall, instead sending the slaves further north, so that the treeline remained a good natural barrier. Many Cannon Towers were erected behind the Farms to the west; these pounded enemies as they tried to break through. Catapults were placed near these Towers to make sure enemy Ballistas did not attack the Towers unmolested. While the Hall was upgraded into a Fortress, an Ogre Mound, an Alchemist, and an Altar of Storms were our final tasks; the buildup had begun in earnest.

Completion of Orders: We assembled a huge group of Ogre-Magi and Catapults for the first wave of the attack, armed with the best possible weapons, armor, and spells, then moved northeast to assault the city from the rear. After we had killed the pitiful forces outside the city walls, Catapults rolled up and smashed a path through to the inside. Enemy units began pouring through, but our Magi with Bloodlust made quick work of them. After briefly entering the walls to draw out defenders, we began producing Sappers back in our settlement, which now had a clear path on which to enter and demolish structures at will with Ogre escorts. Slowly we worked our way westward, removing Towers and Ballistas first and defending our Catapults with troops. Within a short time, the city lay in ruins. At our leisure, we built a Shipyard to take care of any targets beyond the range of our Catapults. The Alliance knew my commander's name now, and soon they would know their Maker as well.

Sappers can blow up mountains as well as enemies.

Mission Ten: The Destruction of Stratholme

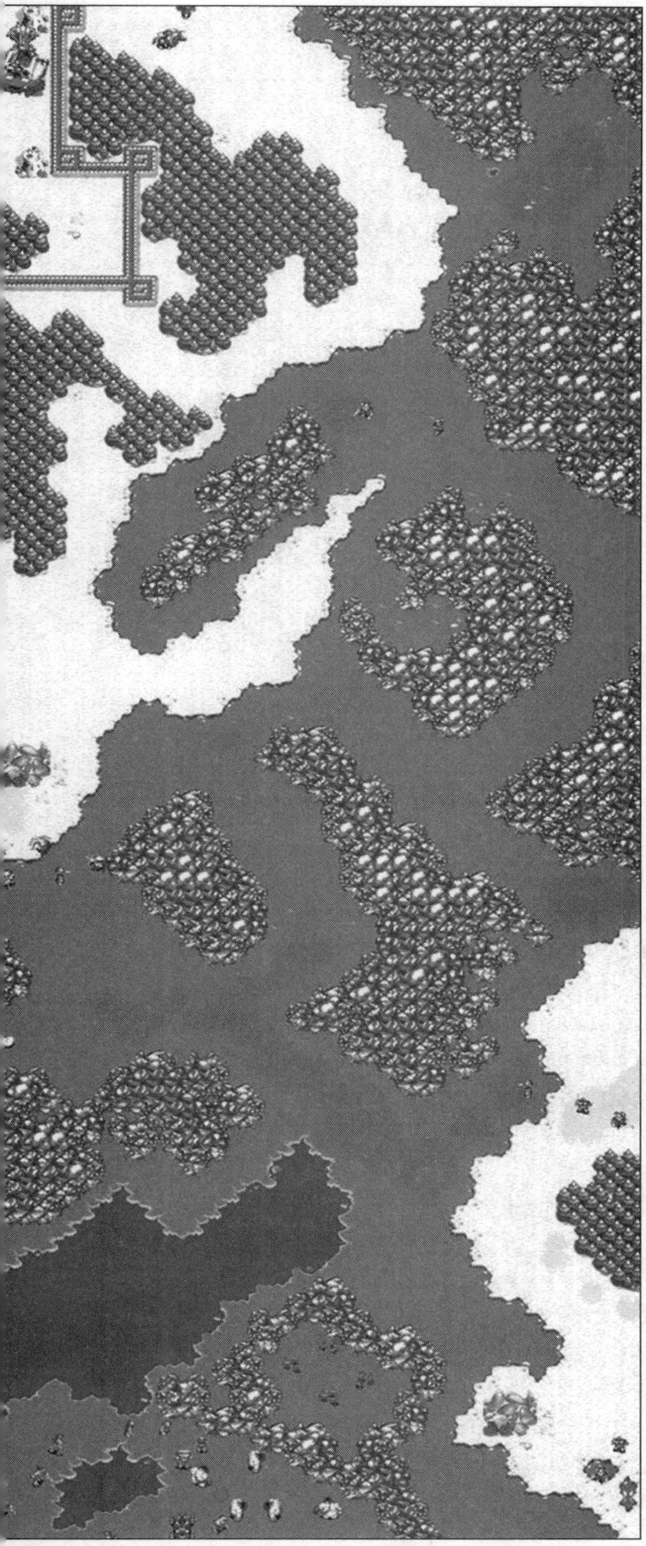

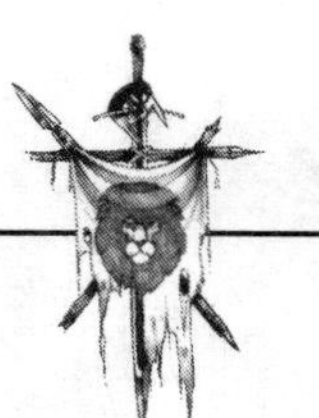

Mission Eleven: The Dead Rise as Quel'thalas Falls

Orders: With the destruction of Stratholme, the Alliance supply lines to Quel'thalas have been severed. Only a handful of Human and Elven defenders remain to safeguard the ancient Elf kingdom from the onslaught of the Horde. The enchanted domain of the Elves has inspired Gul'dan to unleash his most perverted creation—the Death Knights. Formed from the corpses of the fallen Knights of Azeroth, these once-proud defenders of Humanity now serve the Horde in a blasphemous state of eternal undeath. Unleashing dark spells of necromantic horror on their terrified foes, these Death Knights seek to loose their wrath on any foolish enough to stand in their way.

Objective: Destroy the last of the remaining Elven Strongholds.

Preparations for Battle: Since our objective was to remove the Stronghold itself, our plan was to raise a huge force and beat a path through their back door in much the same way as we had at Stratholme. First we needed to secure our base for construction. A group of Alliance enemies were already inside our walls, so the Sappers were quickly moved out of the way for our Ogres to do their work. When all was quiet again, the Ogres immediately marched out through the west entrance and circled around to the other side of the forest, where more Alliance troops were trying to gather. From that point onward, we continued to keep forces in the clearing to eliminate enemies before they had a chance to gather in force there. We then plugged the west entrance with two Farms and began building an army of workers to prepare for the assault.

Methods of Destruction: When we had our Hall built up into a Fortress and complemented with an Ogre Mound, an Altar of Storms, and three Barracks, it was necessary to send workers south to raise another Town Hall near a second mine. A constant stream of Ogre-Magi poured out of our Barracks; a group of them was sent to guard the new Hall while the rest continued to guard the clearing. Sappers were also built in large numbers, for these were the tools with which the enemy Stronghold would easily be demolished. At last we had a huge army of twenty Ogre-Magi, four Cata-

pults, and ten Sappers to begin the final assault. Other Magi stayed in the clearing to defend the base. Our army marched off in force to the southeast corner of the area.

Completion of Orders: After slaughtering the few defenders around a third mine directly east of the city, our Magi gathered west of it near an ice bridge, but did not cross it. Floating Eyes were summoned to look to the west, where a Tower and Ballistas awaited our arrival. The Magi then cast multiple Runes just north of the tower, and then brought in Catapults to start on it. The first barrage prompted the Alliance guards to rush us; they exploded nicely on the Runes we had set for them. Having cleaned up the remaining units, we continued west and demolished a Lumber Mill and a Farm. While we waited for our magic to build up again, the Sappers were brought up, but remained in the rear, as we removed another emplacement of Towers and defenders in the same fashion as the last with Runes doing most of the work for us. From there we made the final push through the back door of the city, pausing to build up Mana again, and set Runes to draw city guards to their deaths.

Set Runes for your enemies, but make sure to remember where they are.

Mission Eleven: The Dead Rise as Quel'thalas Falls

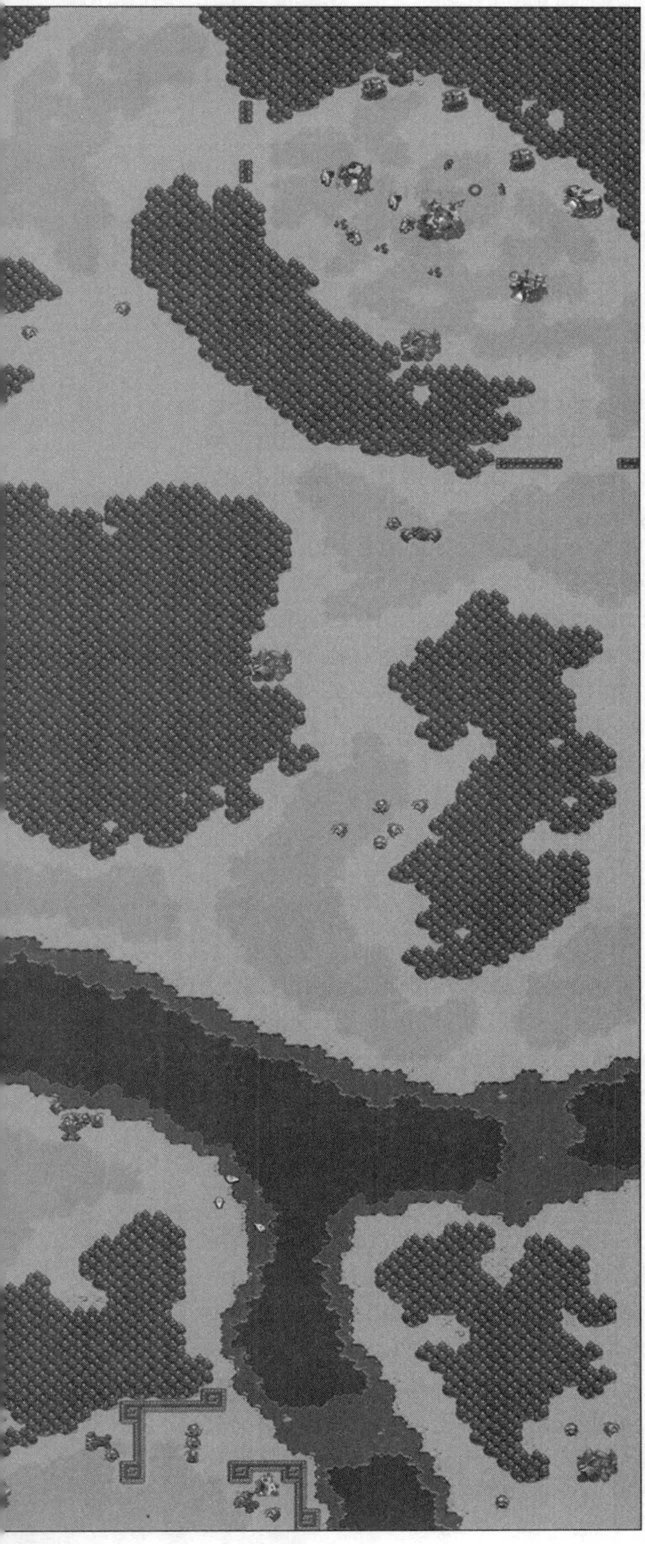

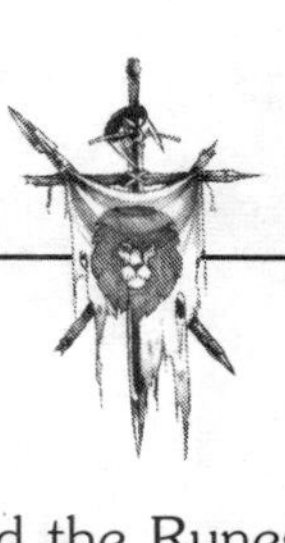

Finally we allowed the Runes that had not gone off to dissipate, cast Bloodlust on our Magi, targeted Towers with our Catapults, and poured into the city to create as much chaos as possible. This cleared the way for our Sappers, who rushed in and leveled the Stronghold with a fantastic display of fire and noise. The rest of the Elves soon retreated, knowing that the Horde could not be stopped. Today, once again, our Gods were pleased.

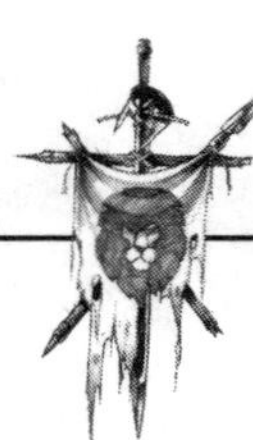

Act IV: The Tides of Darkness

Mission Twelve: The Tomb of Sargeras

Orders: The Northlands have fallen. Now only the western regions of Lordaeron stand defiant before the irresistible might of the Horde. As the Orc clans prepare for their final, massive campaign against the weakening Alliance, the War Chief sends you ill tidings. . . .

Gul'dan and his Stormreaver clan have betrayed the Horde and coerced the Twilight's Hammer clan to set sail and seek an ancient tomb said to be buried beneath the waves. An infiltrator under the direction of Doomhammer reports that Gul'dan has indeed raised volcanic islands from the ocean floor and has thus opened a hidden vault. Though it is unknown what the great Warlock has released from this tomb, the War Chief has issued this command: Destroy the renegade clans and return with the head of Gul'dan.

Objective: Destroy the Stormreaver and Twilight's Hammer clans; slay the Warlock Gul'dan.

Preparations for Battle: First, we had to establish a city on the largest of the islands to the east and north. For this purpose, we sent our warships with a Flier to clear the way. Two enemy ships and a submersible had to be sunk first, then a Tower; finally, the inland Catapult was drawn to shore with a fast Destroyer and disassembled. While the warships waited, the Transports were loaded with all but Sappers and Peons to make a landing; soon the island was ours. While the existing structures were removed, the Transports went back for the rest of the units and brought them safely to shore. From that point it was a matter of building a city from scratch, starting with a Hall as close to the mine as possible without being too close to shore. With the threat of enemy Juggernaughts coming soon, all units were moved as far inland as possible and the ships were sent to anchor at the southern tip of the island.

Methods of Destruction: As soon as a Barracks, a Lumber Mill, and a Blacksmith had been built, we concentrated on producing Catapults. These

we used to sink any enemy ships foolish enough to wander too close to shore by directing all of them to attack at once, then moving them safely back inland. Cannon Towers helped somewhat, but their lack of mobility got them destroyed almost as fast as they could be built. Once we had a fair-sized group of Catapults to fend off ships, construction of the Shipyard and accompanying structures began on the southeast side of the island as far from enemy eyes as possible. To carry out our plan of invasion, we would need only two Juggers and three Transports to make a landing on the main island. We loaded them with five Trolls to give them a chance against flying Daemons, a single Worker, six Ogres, and six Catapults.

COMPLETION OF ORDERS: The flotilla was escorted by a Zeppelin to spot enemy submersibles. It sailed west to the edge of the area before turning north and quietly passing the main island. Then it headed east to find a good landing spot south of a small barren island. The Juggernaughts were sent in first to clear the shore of a Tower and a Catapult before the troops were unloaded behind a small stand of trees. We were careful to unload the Ogres first, with Catapults behind, and Trolls on the other side, since the enemies

Stop the treacherous Gul'dan from unleashing Daemons on his former allies.

Mission Twelve: The Tomb of Sargeras

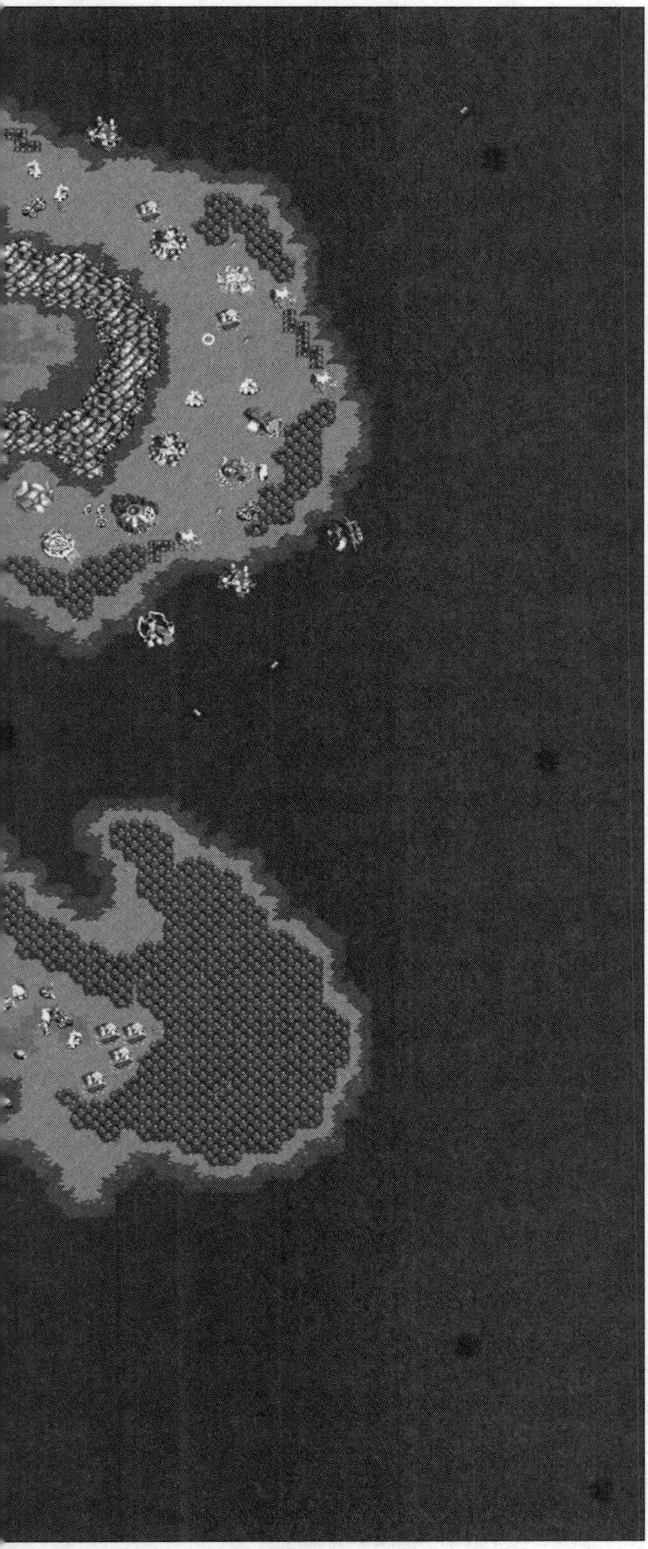

on shore would come to us once the Catapults started on the enemy Barracks nearby. When things quieted down a bit, we erected our own Barracks and began pouring troops and Catapults through it to slowly take over the island. Later we finished Gul'dan and Cho'gall by blowing a path through the rock with Sappers, and claimed both of their heads as a clear signal to all who would oppose the Horde. For that matter, the same treatment was promised to any other clans that questioned our commander's military prowess.

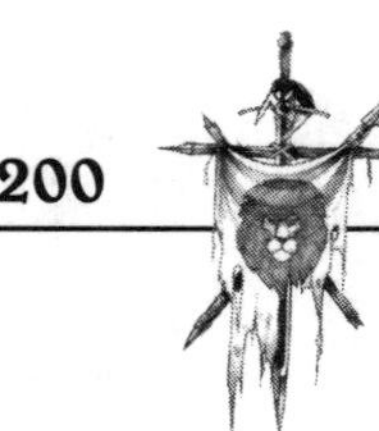

Mission Thirteen: The Siege of Dalaran

Orders: The hour of judgment is close at hand as the Orcish Hordes stand ready to sweep across this domain like a pestilence and seize the capital of Lordaeron. Standing vigilant above the plains, like the descending arm of twilight itself, is the Violet Citadel of Dalaran. The Citadel—serving as sanctum and haven to the Mages of Lordaeron—is the last barrier between the Orcs and their subjugation of Humanity. Manifested in the combined magical prowess of all Mages within the Alliance, this place must fall for the Horde to conquer Lordaeron.

Fortunately, Orgrim Doomhammer has saved his greatest weapon and stands ready to unleash it on the unsuspecting Alliance at just this moment: Dragons.

Objective: Destroy Dalaran and all its defenders.

Preparations for Battle: Dragons indeed would be our main weapon in the conquest of the island, but first we would have to raise a city to support their production. All our military units swept quickly southward and removed all defenders near the mine; the construction of the necessary buildings was begun in earnest. During this time, we erected many Guard Towers to deal with the constant harassment of enemy Gryphons; a Shipyard went up to produce Tankers and Destroyers for the same purpose.

Methods of Destruction: When we started running out of gold, we needed to assault the southern outpost to get Peons beyond it to another mine. The first step of this operation was to send a single Sapper to blow up the western Tower. With this task out of the way, we rolled in Catapults to remove the rest, escorted by more troops, and the way was cleared to start another Hall and plunder its resources. Another Shipyard went up near it, to launch more Destroyers on that side of the land bridge for defense against Gryphons. By that time, we had four Dragon Roosts started. Soon the skies would belong to us.

Completion of Orders: The assault on the island would require the combined efforts of Dragons, Catapults, and Ogres. The Dragons could do most of the destructive work, but Catapults with Ogre escorts were required to take out enemy Guard Towers, which could fire on them. Sappers also came in handy for a few of them, but most structures fell to the Catapults while the Dragons worked on mobile targets. With careful and constant strikes on single targets, each followed by a brief retreat, it was only a matter of time before the island was ours. Very soon now, we would be able to say the same for the rest of this World.

Very little can stop a pack of Dragons.

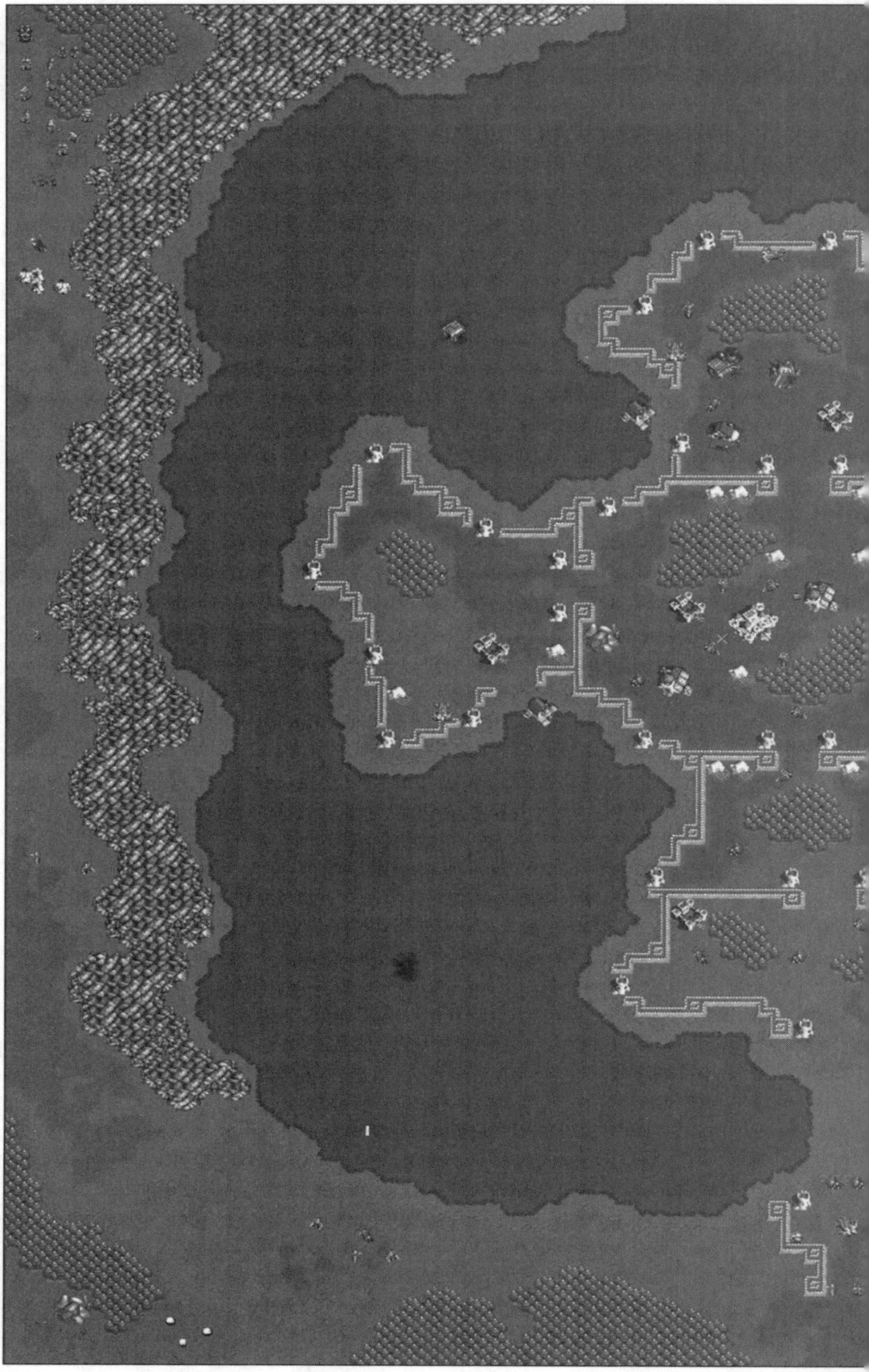

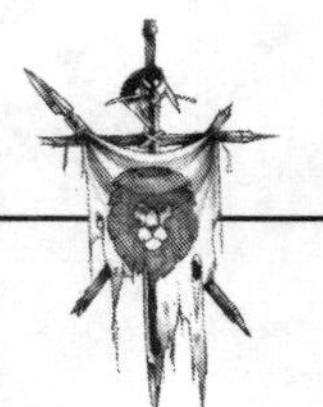

Mission Thirteen: The Siege of Dalaran

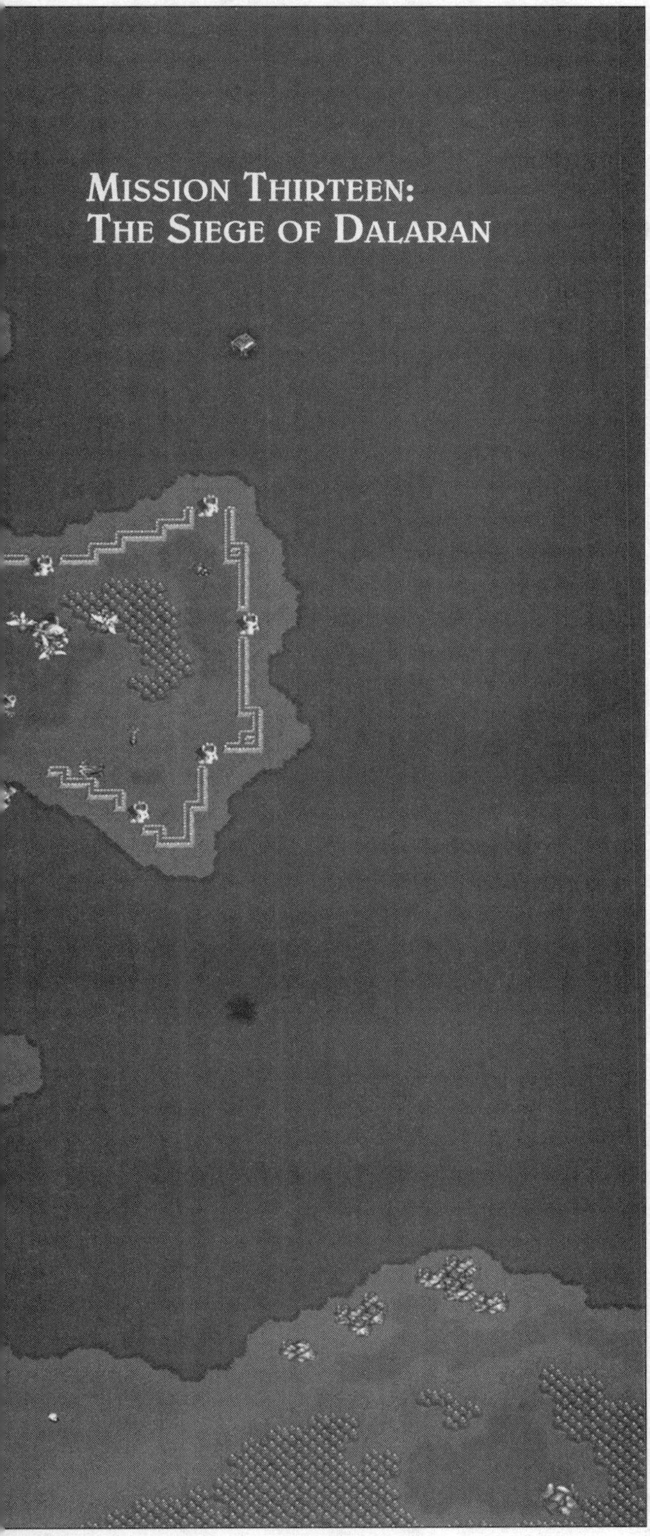

Mission Fourteen: The Fall of Lordaeron

Orders: The alabaster parapets of Lordaeron's capital loom before you in the distance. The proud, defiant armies of the Alliance stand resolute in their final moments. All that remains is the shrill clarion call to battle and the fulfillment of our destiny. The tides of darkness are now at hand!

Objective: Destroy all that you behold in the name of the Horde!

Preparations for Battle: Once again, we would rely on Dragons to sack most of the capital. The most suitable site for the Roosts was on the island where our troops had already made a successful landing. Though we already had a base started, the encampment was doomed to fall to a constant stream of raiders soon, so new construction began near the mine on the island. This site was also far enough inland that only Gryphons could harass us, and these would be taken care of by numerous Guard Towers and Trolls.

Methods of Destruction: All the structures necessary to develop Dragon Roosts were built first. Four Roosts were soon launching the terrible beasts into the air. Once we had about eight of them flying, their first targets were the numerous enemy troops stationed near the center of the island. It was odd that they never organized a land attack; perhaps they were savoring the last hours before their inevitable destruction. Next came their navy, which never stood a chance against so many firebreathers flying together. Though their Destroyers managed to bring down a few, these were replaced quickly. The assault continued with the removal of their Shipyards. A protective circle of Guard Towers made attacks on the center of the capital prohibitively expensive, but little was left to hinder an amphibious landing.

Completion of Orders: While the Dragons had fun incinerating Towers and clearing a wide section of coastline for a landing, we constructed a Shipyard and accompanying structures to produce two Transports. These made a standard assault on the mainland with four Catapults, seven Ogres, and a single Peon to raise a Barracks. The Dragons then concentrated on mobile units, while the Catapults methodically removed stationary targets near shore and later focused on the Guard Towers so our reptiles could start on the interior.

It was all too easy. I now believe that it is our right and destiny to devour this World.

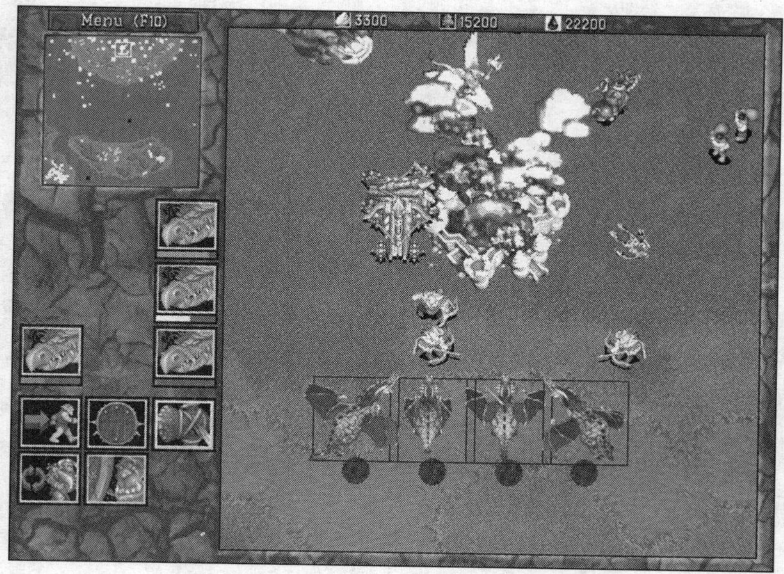

The fall of Lordaeron's capital.

Mission Fourteen: The Fall of Lordaeron

METZEN • 95

Chapter Five

Methods of Madness

"In time,
his victories could not easily be counted. . . ."
—Conan the Barbarian

The leadership of any army, great or small, determines whether or not the army will live to fight another day. This chapter not only describes the simple and effective deployment of troops, but also the secret tactics that immortalize great generals in song and legend.

STANDARD TACTICS

These strategies are designed to work in almost any situation, and encompass the majority of effective operations in both single- and multiple-player games. Used as a foundation, this advice ensures that you will survive long enough to apply the more advanced tricks in the latter section.

GATHERING RESOURCES

The first and most important key to quickly gathering gold is to keep a clear path between the Hall and the mine. Placing structures directly beside or even one space away from either of these will cause the workers to emerge on the wrong side, or stop altogether if they walk into a bottleneck. Worse still is a situation that forces them to choose a longer route, often taking them outside the town where they become fair game for enemies lingering out of range of your defenses. Players busy with military concerns cannot afford to spend time making sure their workers are doing their job, because the smooth and constant flow of gold is vital to an effective buildup.

Since there are usually several mines on any given map, try sending a lone worker and a few combat units to set up a secondary Hall close to another mine. Assuming it remains unmolested for a time, new workers can be trained on the spot and begin gathering gold to double or triple your rate of income. If the mine has a large amount of gold in it, consider building Towers or another Barracks nearby to ensure the survival of your workers. This also provides a backup plan if your primary village gets sacked.

When gathering lumber, pay close attention to exactly where your workers are getting it from. A line of trees is a very effective natural barrier, and cutting holes in it will only allow more enemies to pour through. Since workers are dim and will start cutting wherever it is convenient after their initial orders, make sure to send them to forests without any strategic significance, even if it means doing so outside of town. In this case, send soldiers to help defend them while they work. Losing a few workers is far less damaging than an assault on your structures, because you can always train more if the remainder concentrates on gold instead. Finally, whenever possible, build Lumber Mills as close to the cutting as possible to greatly speed the gathering process.

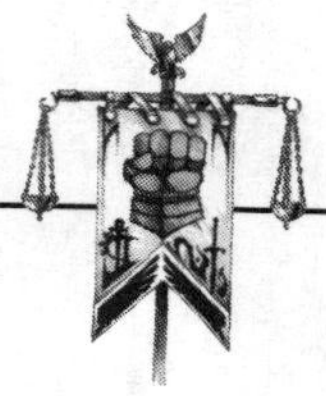

Building Cities

It is of utmost importance that the city be able to defend itself from enemy raids as soon as possible. Quickly inspect the surrounding territory, and determine where enemies are most likely to invade from. At these spots, first build Farms to block passage, or start a defensive line of Farms that form a wall. Farms have considerably more hit points than Towers or walls, and will take much more time to get through. Directly behind these Farms, place one or two Towers or several Archers/Trolls to pelt enemies lined up before the barrier, and from that point you need not worry about invasions from that particular direction. Often, only Farms are necessary to cause enemies to take a longer path, since the computer chooses the shortest open path to their destination and Farms are usually not a primary target.

The next step to planning an efficient city is to decide which units will be needed to accomplish your goals, and build only the structures required to produce them. As previously mentioned, the most effective attacks are conducted with large numbers of basic units; the more resources you have available to devote to them, the greater the number of active units. Building a second or third Barracks is also highly recommended, because players often have more gold than time available. Spending huge amounts of effort to get Dragons into the air might all be in vain if the city gets overrun in the process. Establish a strong city and army before devoting attention to specialized units.

Land Attacks

Safety in numbers is the key to success in any situation, and the ability to issue orders to nine units at a time allows them to decimate single opponents. Always assign a portion of your forces to concentrate on one enemy at a time, because half-dead adversaries still do the same amount of damage as perfectly healthy ones. The computer makes a habit of engaging either the closest convenient target or one that attacked first, then pounding it to death before moving on to the next. Keep your units tagged and gathered together, or else they will run off chasing retreating foes and end up getting killed when they separate from the pack.

When commanding a mixed group of units, always keep those with one-space attacks in front of those with missile weapons. One of the most effective coordinated assaults involves the use of many Knights or Ogres in front of a few Ballistas or Catapults. Mobile computer enemies will often target more powerful units if given a choice, and when they come calling, your fighters can easily cut them down while the war wagons launch missiles at stationary structures. When taking out Towers, order all of your Catapults/Ballistas to attack from a distance and they will stop at their maximum range before firing. Although they will be out of range of even Cannon Towers, your faster units will be subject to bombardment if they wander just one space ahead. Therefore, order them to stand their ground on either side, and let advancing defenders get a few hits in until the Tower falls first.

Marine Tactics

A quick inspection of cost-versus-firepower of warships shows a decided advantage in building Juggernaughts and Battleships rather than Destroyers. (However, keep in mind that only Destroyers can target flying units such as Dragons.) Submersibles are also nice, but are too easy to sink once detected. A flotilla of tall warships escorted by a Flier can decimate not only all other vessels, but their extended cannon range allows heavy bombardment of many land targets as well.

However, having at least one fast Destroyer does come in very handy for leading enemy Catapults/Ballistas closer to shore, while the main group waits safely out of range before attacking all at once. For that matter, even a Transport or a Tanker can serve the purpose of baiting mobile enemies to shore, as long as you do not need them for more important tasks.

Amphibious landings should always utilize at least two fully loaded Transports, escorted by as many warships as possible to clear the beach head. A standard landing party should consist mostly of melee units, supported by two or three Catapults/Ballistas for long-range fire. Where an extended campaign on foreign soil is expected, bring along at least one worker to immediately throw a Barracks up. Enemies will concentrate on the new structure, which has considerably more armor and hit points than any single combat unit, letting your own forces concentrate on the attackers. After an

initial cost of resources, the structure continually "heals" itself without further cost; even if they manage to destroy it before construction is complete, it at least draws fire away from your armies.

An Elemental Relationship

One key strategy to keep in mind is the relationship between land, sea, and air units.

Archers/Axethrowers, Mages/Death Knights, and Guard Towers are the only land units that can attack air units.

The Destroyer is the only ship that can attack air units.

Only flying units, Subs/Turtles, and Towers can spot Submarines.

For example, a group of Battleships with a Flying Machine will completely annihilate anything that sails the seas or runs along the coast. But even a single Dragon will wreak havoc because none of the mighty ships can fire back.

Tips, Tactics, and Secrets!

Whether you are playing custom scenarios or any of the campaign missions delineated in Chapters 3 and 4, certain strategies remain constant. In the paragraphs that follow, you will be given many tools with which to enhance your command abilities. Use them well and wisely to mold an unstoppable force.

- If you have Peasants/Peons *repair* a building under construction, it will be completed much faster. A second Peasant makes the completion twice as fast, three Peasants are three times as fast, and so on.
- Casting Invisibility on Transports makes them quite effective. Unfortunately, if you select a Transport and tell it to unload all its troops, it will become visible. However, if you select the individual unit's *portrait* to unload it, the Transport will remain invisible. This allows a great covert operation on the enemy's shoreline where your units just seem to appear—try this with Bombers!

- If you are being attacked by a clump of units, cast a Flame Shield on the center unit. This will begin to cause damage to all units around that one. It will also cause your opponent to spend time moving his units away from the flamed one instead of attacking you.
- Bomber and Sapper units can be used to clear terrain. Tell them to detonate a forest or rock hex; when they explode, they remove a hefty chunk. This is useful for craftily creating a pathway into enemy territory.
- Cast Invisibility and Flame Shield on a Destroyer and wreak havoc on your enemy's naval fleets. Destroyers are exceptionally quick and cannot be hit since they will never become visible (the Flame Shield is doing the damage, not the invisible unit).
- Build Towers in an opponent's city to create a great deal of chaos quickly. If you can get them up and upgraded quickly, they will start to open up on everything within range!
- Exorcism will damage both Skeletons *and* Death Knights.
- Cast Unholy Armor on a Death Knight, then cast Death and Decay on that Death Knight. This is a tremendously effective way to kill a large number of enemies who come to kill the Death Knight. Talk about an effective distraction!
- Cast Runes on the ground between a Gold Mine and the enemy's Town Hall; this will greatly disrupt his economy.
- Use your Catapults to take out Towers; their range is slightly greater than that of a tower.
- To get the first shot on a Tower with a Destroyer or Battleship, order the ship to move toward the Tower. The Tower will fire and will generally miss the moving target. Then immediately order the ship to attack the Tower. It will stop and fire, thus giving you the first hit.
- Have your flying units follow your Destroyers and Battleships, so they can easily spot any Submarines or Giant Turtles. This will save you from having to group them with the ships, thus allowing you to move even more than nine units.

- If you are attacked and have only Peons, make sure to group them and have them attack a single opponent. The damage they do is small, but it does add up.
- Use your Death Knight to cast Death Coil on a group of enemy units. When they come after the Death Knight, immediately cast Death and Decay between them and you. If you can bring up a second Death Knight, he can cast Death and Decay immediately behind the advancing enemy, cutting them off from their usual safe retreat.
- Sending your Bombers and Sappers into large groups can kill several enemies at one time. Also, telling your Bombers or Sappers to detonate between two buildings will damage both. This is very effective for taking out Farms.
- Destroying enemy Farms can cripple their ability to produce more units in a siege.
- Do *not* group select Bombers and Sappers and give them one target. They will arrive at the same time, and the first to detonate will kill the others before they can damage the target.
- You will need to keep Dragons and Gryphons spaced apart or they will risk hitting each other and damaging themselves. A good tactic is to send a single Dragon or Gryphon in among a large group of enemy Dragons or Gryphons and watch them damage each other.
- If your opponent seems to build a great number of sea vessels, start concentrating on Dragons or Gryphons. Not only can they damage ships, but your opponent's land defenses will probably not be as well developed if he has been concentrating on the seas.
- In a narrow river area, you can use a Peon to create a Shipyard and then immediately cancel the build. He will pop out of the canceled building on the opposite shore. This is a quick way to get across to enemy territory or to flee from enemies so you can start up another Town Hall. Also, you can put a Transport in a narrow area and use it as a bridge for units (having them get on and off). Try choosing different places to build Shipyards and different ways to best use the terrain as a natural defense.

- Move a Sub or a Turtle under an untapped oil patch. When the enemy's Oil Transport comes exploring, he's in for a surprise!
- Whenever you ally yourself with another player, put either a unit you can afford to lose or a Tower in his town. If he chooses to remove you as an ally, you will have advance warning immediately when your unit is attacked.
- Slow is a great counter for Bomber squads—it gives your units the ability to get to them before they can do damage. Similarly, casting Haste on your Sappers will get them in much faster than your opponent expects.
- In a two- or three-player game with medium or high resources selected, build a Farm, a Barracks, and as many Grunts as possible *without* building a Town Hall. Then send out your troops and find the enemy before he can get an economy going. This will work *only* in a two- or three-player game—with more players than that, you may get the quick kill, but you will soon be fodder.
- Casting Speed on Catapults makes for a very fast and fierce attack squad.
- Whirlwinds and Runes are highly effective for killing Peasants or Peons. Whirlwinds are very effective when cast on Barracks because they immediately damage any unit being produced. Multiple Whirlwinds can be devastating to a town and its Tower defenses.
- Troll Berserkers with Regenerate are great for tactical battles where rotating your troops is a strategy. Their ability to heal themselves is a great benefit in running battles.
- Raise Dead is effective when you are planning an assault on Peasants or Peons. Not only do you destroy your opponent's economy, but you then use his own people against him.
- Peons and Peasants are effective when you are scouting an enemy's lands. If you are attacked or approached, they can immediately build a Barracks or a Tower, making them as strong as the building. This assumes that you have enough resources, of course.

- Although the time and effort to develop Rangers is costly, upgrading their arrows to their maximum strength allows them to inflict as much or more average damage as a Guard Tower. A row of Rangers set to receive a charge can decimate anything that steps within their range, which is also longer with the appropriate training.

Cheat Codes

Cheat	Code
Victory	Unite the clans
Loss	You pitiful worm
God	It is a good day to die
Cash	Glittering prizes
Oil	Valdez
Magic	Every little thing she does
Upgrade	Deck me out
Show Map	On Screen
Fast Build	Make it so
Finale	There can be only one
No Victory	Never a winner
Lumber	Hatchet, axe and saw
Enable Mission Jump	Tigerlily
Jump to Mission	Orc 14, Human 14, etc.

Appendix

Warcraft II Multiplayer Strategies

Indeed, one of the praiseworthy attributes of Warcraft II is that the game allows multiple players to wage war against each other. This presents Warcraft II players with myriad strategic options other than simply striving to defeat the computer. The following appendix details strategies that can prove to be the difference between victory and defeat on the sometimes crowded and ever-more competitive multiplayer battlefield.

While many of the strategies outlined in the appendix may also apply to players pitting their wits against the computer, they are intended to facilitate multiplayer efforts.

The appendix is divided into five sections: Allies, Options, Combat, Buildings, and Multiplayer Custom Scenarios.

Allies

Choose Your Allies

Before you begin the game, discussing who you will ally with can be very beneficial. Make sure that both you and your allies select each other in the Ally menu as soon as possible, so no accidental contact occurs between you that could result in an attack.

Pick Different Races

If there are two or more allies on the same side, they should pick opposing races (one Human and one Orc, etc.). This ensures that the allied parties will have the widest selection of spells available to them. On the other hand, if they choose the same races, they will both have the exact same benefits—and weaknesses. When mixed up, the allied parties can help defend one another, diluting their combined weaknesses and supporting their strengths.

Allied Victory?

It is important to discuss with your ally what your goals are: Will you share the spoils of victory, or battle each other for ultimate supremacy? For instance, if you plan on clobbering all of your opponents en route to a *team victory*, but your ally thinks that the two of you will fight for the ultimate prize, he may have developed a strategy from the start to defeat you in the end. In the meantime, you were simply concentrating on the enemies.

Communication

Another benefit of having allies is that, through communication, you can discover more about territory in a mission map than you could on your own. This helps you decide the best locations to place your buildings. For instance, if you know that your ally is east of you, and the only other significant opening for attacking your forces is to the west, you can focus all defenses on the west side. (Of course, that's assuming you can trust your ally.)

Coordinating an Attack

Continuously communicate with your allies. Knowing that your ally has sent four Paladins to aid your Death Knights in a raid could very well decide whether you launch the attack. Furthermore, when coordinating an attack, let your ally know what you are sending, and where. This will allow him to send some of his troops for support. And don't forget to reciprocate the favor when the time comes—unless you have your own dark plans....

Options

Race

Although each race can hold its own against another, choosing one race leads to a slightly different mode of play. A real-life player often has the ability to accentuate the differences (see below) and develop unique game play with each one.

Humans

The healing abilities of the Human Paladin is very beneficial in siege attacks. Send units forward, then retreat, heal, and send again, rotating different lines of attack with plenty of Paladins to sustain healing power. Also, the Exorcism (for Paladins) and Polymorph (for Human Mages) spells are very effective, the latter even from a distance, and both spells are especially useful against the more powerful creatures of the Horde. Even when the God cheat is enabled, these spells can cause mass destruction! Also, Blizzard and Flame Shield are very useful ambush spells for the Human Mage.

Orcs

The Ogre Magi spell Runes is highly effective at guarding entrances and/or exits. It is also a great spell to use to begin an ambush. Death Knights also have a solid set of spells, with Death and Decay allowing them to inflict destruction on multiple units at a one time. In fact, Death and Decay works well in conjunction with the Ogre Magi's Runes spell. Draw another player

Warcraft II on the Internet

Want to play Warcraft II over the Internet? Yes, the Internet provides yet another battlefield for Warcraft II fans with the help of a software program called KALI.

For more information about KALI, visit the KALI home page on the World Wide Web at www.axxis.com/kali, or contact the program's author, Jay Cotton, at jay@kali.net.

A patch that improves the performance of Warcraft II when played over KALI can be downloaded from Blizzard Entertainment's website at www.blizzard.com. The patch is provided as a free service to Internet users. It is not a Blizzard Entertainment supported product. Please do not contact Blizzard technical support about this patch.

into attacking you and, when he triggers the Runes spell, quickly lay a Death and Decay spell behind him, forcing him forward into, hopefully, an onslaught of devastating Runes spells.

Resources

For a beginning player, you may want to select High resources to make life a little easier. You will be able to build more units and buildings at the onset

when your mining operation is at its lowest level of production. By the time you run out of gold, your mining operation should be running fairly smoothly.

Cheats Enabled

Whether you enable cheats will depend on how much experience you have at Warcraft II. You should probably leave it disabled until you have learned how to operate the game's controls efficiently, since enabled cheats affect everyone, and a more seasoned player, or, worse yet, the computer, will be able to make much better use of the cheats than a beginner. Likewise, you definitely should not use the God cheat, although the Harvest cheat can come in handy at times.

Tileset

Other than aesthetics, there isn't much difference in game play here. One neat thing to point out is that critters will change between the tilesets.

Units

For multiplayer games with beginners, use the default mode for units. Some of the scenarios will have buildings pre-made for you, so you can develop certain more advanced units quicker. However, if you have experienced players, starting with only one peon will give you more flexibility with your game development.

Fog of War

This is an option you should definitely leave on. A lot of the new features in Warcraft II, such as flying machines/zeppelins, lose something of their value and most of their fun when this feature is left off. Also, the range of sight via these flying devices is also less valuable if you have Fog of War off. It will make the game easier, as you can develop one flying machine and easily send it across an entire map, but you lose a little excitement without it.

Starting Locations

If you start at a random location, you may or may not land anywhere near a decent starting point. Conversely, starting at a fixed location will generally land you within a few steps of a mine. Until you are confident enough in your ability to locate a decent place to mine, you should begin at a fixed location.

However, if you begin the game with High resources, you don't have to necessarily start at a fixed location to succeed early. You can actually create a town that is nowhere near a mine, protect it, then send your peon (along with a few guards) to find a good mine, and begin developing a second town. This strategy can be beneficial if you are playing with allies and aim to link your cities together quickly. (You both will have a longer line to defend, however.) If fairly close to your ally in proximity, this strategy also gives you both a greater area of protection in which to develop units and buildings.

Combat

Offensive Tactics

Know the Layout of the Land

Before you can mount a decent attack, you need to know the lay of the land before you. Unless you are the gung-ho type (all brawn and no brains) who charges directly into battle, you'd probably like to save as many of your units as you can, and learning the lay of the land you're about to wage war on can accomplish this.

Performing advanced scouting on the land awaiting you can be done easily with a Flying Machine/Zeppelin, or by sending out cheap scouts like Peasants, who can draw deadly fire away from your actual fighting forces. For instance, send Peasants to build a Scout Tower right in the middle of the enemy camp (or as close as you can get). The Scout Tower won't last as long as a Farm or Barracks, but, once built, the visual range it provides you will be invaluable in determining how many nearby reinforcements the enemies have. And if it gets upgraded to a Guard or Cannon Tower, it not

only allows you to see the enemy, but it also can initiate an attack upon them as well.

Coordinated Attacks

Once you locate an enemy, let your allies know immediately. Then, plan an attack formation best suited for your combined protection as well as the destruction of your enemy.

For example, if planning to attack an island fortress, both you and your ally should load a Transport or two with Archers/Axe Throwers, Paladins/Ogre-Magi, and Mages/Death Knights. Follow by sending a Destroyer and Battleship to protect the Transport(s). (If you can supply more protection, do it). Next, send a Flying Machine/Zeppelin ahead to search out your enemy's location. Set a trap or two for him, and see if you can bait him into following you. The computer falls for traps regularly, but a human opponent may not, so you will probably have to be the aggressor. Lay down some cover fire with your Archers, Axe Throwers, and ships, then send the Paladins and Ogre-Magi to engage the enemy hand-to-hand. If you brought Catapults or Ballistas as well, let them assist in providing cover.

Concentrate on the enemy's more powerful units and magic-users, and keep your Mages and Death Knights busy casting spells such as Slow and Haste. (You can cast these cheaper spells many times before needing rest.) This will help your melee fighters get in many more attacks per round than their opponents. Also, have your Ogre-Magi cast Bloodlust on each other and the Paladins just before they actually engage the enemy. Finally, if you are a good distance away, a nice Blizzard can help destroy a large number of enemies.

Defensive Tactics

Create a Lifeline

If possible, create a lifeline to your allies as early as you can. Line the pathway with Footmen and Archers (or their equivalents). Have your ally do the same, and you will meet twice as quickly. Once you have met up with each other, begin developing more powerful units and lining the lifeline with both them and Towers (Guard and Cannon, if financially possible). With both you

and your Ally responsible for maintaining the lifeline, it should require only minimal upkeep.

Ally-Aid

Often times, your allies need aid when you can ill-afford to send it—at the very beginning of the game. Nonetheless, sending any units you can spare will usually be enough for your ally to survive. Most allies do remember your efforts, too.

Here's something else to keep in mind—sending even a lone Footman to the aid of you ally allows you to view many portions of the particular mission map you're playing. You will often run into another gold mine en route to your ally. If you happen to have sent a Peasant along, you can build a new Town Hall even closer to your ally, while still reaping all the benefits of having already completed one Town Hall.

Buildings

Town Hall

Build this first. Place it as close (unobstructed) to the mine as possible. Don't worry about the forest; you will place a lumber mill close to it. The mill produces more lumber (+25) and can be placed away from the hall and mine, not obstructing the path of miners.

Farms

You will need one of these second (assuming you started with only a peasant). Develop as many farms as you can quickly. They are great for defense, and with excess food, you can develop armies at will as opposed to needing to build a farm in the middle of a battle to create reinforcements. This can be the difference between winning and losing a battle.

Towers

Set these up to block key areas, and upgrade them as soon as possible. Setting them *behind* farms tends to work the best, but be prepared to devote units to repairs in the heat of battle.

Lumber Mills

Place your Lumber Mill right up against the trees if you can, and your Peasants will have a shorter distance to travel to process lumber. Keep the mill away from your Town Hall, however, because the continual traffic between the mine and the forest could cause congestion and leave several Peasants carrying their load and not going anywhere.

Barracks

These structures should be placed near your main exit (they require the least amount of time to move, if the need arises). They need to be built quickly, so you can begin producing Footmen and Archers to protect your budding city before it is capable of producing heavier artillery.

Blacksmiths

Blacksmiths are the benefactors of the whole army. They are capable of upgrading most of the basic units, making them much more powerful. The upgrades are permanent at a one-time cost, so a Blacksmith is well worth the investment. One of the best aspects about the upgrades is that, often times your opponent will be busy building a large army to conquer you, but you have spent your money on upgrading the few you have. With just a little luck, you can overpower your enemies quickly enough to bring them down before they even grow enough in size to do you in.

Gnomish Inventors

These little guys are great for both land and sea campaigns. They allow you to construct Submarines and Flying Machines. A great tactic with a Submarine is to send the vessel along the coasts of enemy islands, steering clear of enemy Towers. The Submarine is all but invisible to most units, except airborne units and Towers, so it can attack from the sea from relative safety. Remember that Submarines cannot attack land or air units.

Stables

Stables are necessary if you are planning a major land-based attack. They allow the production of Knights, the honorable and powerful cavalry of your army. However, if you are planning on making most of your attacks at sea, concentrate your efforts on erecting another building.

Foundries and Refineries

Both are necessary if you plan on seafaring. Without Refineries, your Oil Tankers will process slightly slower, making you wait longer to add units to your army. Foundries also will allow you to upgrade weapons and armor of your armada, essentially making a smaller waterborne force more effective and less visible than a larger, unmodified one.

Church

The Paladin is researched here. Known for their healing abilities, Paladins are the epitome of honor and courage. They will ride into battle to lay their healing hands on a fellow soldier, often absorbing enemy attacks in the process.

Additionally, you should not overlook the Paladin if you are building a fleet of ships or an air force. With a Transport to ferry him where he needs to go, he can often extend the life of a Gryphon Rider who had the bad luck to meet with several Axe Throwers.

Mage Tower

The Mages are costly to summon, but once they have been upgraded with a full contingent of spells, they can be the most devastating of all the units. With their Polymorph spell, they can transform even the most powerful units to passive seals or sheep. In a siege on a town, their Blizzard spell can cause a ton of chaos, especially for units left in the open. Your opponent will often send a large party to find and attack you after being hit with a Blizzard, so be ready with an ambush!

Gryphon Aviary

The most expensive units to summon, Gryphon Aviaries are also one of the most versatile. However, the 2,500 gold pieces price tag can often make people shy away from building them, especially when the route to making an Aviary available is also very expensive and fairly slow. For this reason alone, your may want to reconsider having a full air force as opposed to just a couple of Gryphons to back up your naval fleet.

If you are lucky, your opponent will concentrate all his resources on producing Gryphons. If he does, produce a lot of Rangers and Guard Towers—they are both cheaper and can damage an avian air force. If you notice him not producing a lot of units, he may be saving to produce Gryphons, so you may want to get to his land first. Also, Gryphons damage anything in their path when they fire, and you can sometimes trick them into killing their own people by maneuvering your men between them.

Multiplayer Custom Scenarios

One of the greatest things about Warcraft II is the ability to create your own scenarios. You can edit everything from the map, to the unit values, to sounds. It does take a significant amount of time and effort to create a quality scenario, but when it is finished, it is well worth the effort. By editing the units, you can simulate features such as low morale (by making the units slower and weaker), and even make units superhumanly powerful.

Playing Custom .PUD Files

Single-player .PUD files:

- Go to single-player
- Select Custom Scenario
- Choose Select Scenario
- Set Scenario type to Custom
- Choose the .PUD file you wish to play.

When you create a custom .PUD file make sure it is saved in the Warcraft II directory (i.e., C:\WAR2). This is the default directory for the map editor.

Multiplayer .PUD files (from the multiplayer setup screen):

- Select Custom Scenario
- Choose Select Scenario
- Set Scenario type to Custom
- Choose the .PUD file you wish to play.
- If you have included computer players in your .PUD file, be sure to remember which players (i.e., Player One (Red), Player Two (Blue), etc.) you set up as computer enemies so that you can set them up as computer opponents in the multiplayer setup screen.

First Contact Scenario

Here's an example of a custom scenario to tackle: when the Horde forces are just coming through the Portal. The Orcs are powerful and bloodthirsty, and they have prepared for attack by praying to their dark gods for unholy strength. The Humans are caught off guard, but not completely unaware. Raise the Orcish units' damage and hit points, but give them limited resources. Give the Humans plenty of resources and structures, but a limited amount of starting units. This gives the game a whole new level of play for both teams, as they both have to deal with severe shortcomings. There should be an equal number of players on both sides, with no more than two people allied together (to simulate the arrogance of each kingdom, and the chaotic nature of the Orcs). Try it out!

Computer Game Books

1942: The Pacific Air War—The Official Strategy Guide	$19.95
The 11th Hour: The Official Strategy Guide	$19.95
The 7th Guest: The Official Strategy Guide	$19.95
Aces Over Europe: The Official Strategy Guide	$19.95
Across the Rhine: The Official Strategy Guide	$19.95
Alone in the Dark 3: The Official Strategy Guide	$19.95
Armored Fist: The Official Strategy Guide	$19.95
Ascendancy: The Official Strategy Guide	$19.95
Blackthorne: The Official Strategy Guide	$14.95
CD-ROM Games Secrets, Volume 1	$19.95
Celtic Tales: Balor of the Evil Eye—The Official Strategy Guide	$19.95
Cyberia: The Official Strategy Guide	$19.95
Computer Adventure Games Secrets	$19.95
Descent: The Official Strategy Guide	$19.95
DOOM Battlebook	$14.95
DOOM II: The Official Strategy Guide	$19.95
Dracula Unleashed: The Official Strategy Guide & Novel	$19.95
Dragon Lore: The Official Strategy Guide	$19.95
Dungeon Master II: The Legend of Skullkeep—The Official Strategy Guide	$19.95
Fleet Defender: The Official Strategy Guide	$19.95
Frankenstein: Through the Eyes of the Monster—The Official Strategy Guide	$19.95
Front Page Sports Football Pro '95: The Official Playbook	$19.95
Hell: A Cyberpunk Thriller—The Official Strategy Guide	$19.95
Heretic: The Official Strategy Guide	$19.95
I Have No Mouth, and I Must Scream: The Official Strategy Guide	$19.95
In The 1st Degree: The Official Strategy Guide	$19.95
The Journeyman Project 2: Buried in Time—The Official Strategy Guide	$19.95
Kingdom: The Far Reaches—The Official Strategy Guide	$14.95
King's Quest VII: The Unauthorized Strategy Guide	$19.95
The Legend of Kyrandia: The Official Strategy Guide	$19.95
Lords of Midnight: The Official Strategy Guide	$19.95
Machiavelli the Prince: Official Secrets & Solutions	$12.95
Marathon: The Official Strategy Guide	$19.95
Master of Orion: The Official Strategy Guide	$19.95
Master of Magic: The Official Strategy Guide	$19.95
Microsoft Arcade: The Official Strategy Guide	$12.95
Microsoft Flight Simulator 5.1: The Official Strategy Guide	$19.95

Microsoft Golf: The Official Strategy Guide	$19.95
Microsoft Space Simulator: The Official Strategy Guide	$19.95
Might and Magic Compendium: The Authorized Strategy Guide for Games I, II, III, and IV	$19.95
Myst: The Official Strategy Guide	$19.95
Online Games: In-Depth Strategies and Secrets	$19.95
Oregon Trail II: The Official Strategy Guide	$19.95
Outpost: The Official Strategy Guide	$19.95
The Pagemaster: Official CD-ROM Strategy Guide	$14.95
Panzer General: The Official Strategy Guide	$19.95
Perfect General II: The Official Strategy Guide	$19.95
Prince of Persia: The Official Strategy Guide	$19.95
Prisoner of Ice: The Official Strategy Guide	$19.95
Rebel Assault: The Official Insider's Guide	$19.95
Return to Zork Adventurer's Guide	$14.95
Romance of the Three Kingdoms IV: Wall of Fire—The Official Strategy Guide	$19.95
Shadow of the Comet: The Official Strategy Guide	$19.95
Sid Meier's Civilization, or Rome on 640K a Day	$19.95
Sid Meier's Colonization: The Official Strategy Guide	$19.95
SimCity 2000: Power, Politics, and Planning	$19.95
SimEarth: The Official Strategy Guide	$19.95
SimFarm Almanac: The Official Guide to SimFarm	$19.95
SimLife: The Official Strategy Guide	$19.95
SimTower: The Official Strategy Guide	$19.95
SubWar 2050: The Official Strategy Guide	$19.95
Terry Pratchett's Discworld: The Official Strategy Guide	$19.95
TIE Fighter: The Official Strategy Guide	$19.95
TIE Fighter: Defender of the Empire—Official Secrets & Solutions	$12.95
Thunderscape: The Official Strategy Guide	$19.95
Ultima: The Avatar Adventures	$19.95
Ultima VII and Underworld: More Avatar Adventures	$19.95
Under a Killing Moon: The Official Strategy Guide	$19.95
WarCraft: Orcs & Humans Official Secrets & Solutions	$9.95
Warlords II Deluxe: The Official Strategy Guide	$19.95
Wing Commander I, II, and III: The Ultimate Strategy Guide	$19.95
X-COM Terror From The Deep: The Official Strategy Guide	$19.95
X-COM UFO Defense: The Official Strategy Guide	$19.95
X-Wing: Collector's CD-ROM—The Official Strategy Guide	$19.95

VIDEO GAME BOOKS

3DO Game Guide	$16.95
Battle Arena Toshinden Game Secrets: The Unauthorized Edition	$12.95
Behind the Scenes at Sega: The Making of a Video Game	$14.95
Boogerman Official Game Secrets	$12.95
Breath of Fire Authorized Game Secrets	$14.95
Complete Final Fantasy III Forbidden Game Secrets	$14.95
Donkey Kong Country Game Secrets the Unauthorized Edition	$9.95
EA SPORTS Official Power Play Guide	$12.95
Earthworm Jim Official Game Secrets	$12.95
Killer Instinct Game Secrets: The Unauthorized Edition	$9.95
The Legend of Zelda: A Link to the Past—Game Secrets	$12.95
Lord of the Rings Official Game Secrets	$12.95
Maximum Carnage Official Game Secrets	$9.95
Mega Man X Official Game Secrets	$14.95
Mortal Kombat II Official Power Play Guide	$9.95
NBA JAM: The Official Power Play Guide	$12.95
GamePro Presents: Nintendo Games Secrets Greatest Tips	$11.95
Nintendo Games Secrets, Volumes 1, 2, 3, and 4	$11.95 each
Ogre Battle: The March of the Black Queen—The Official Power Play Guide	$14.95
Parent's Guide to Video Games	$12.95
Secret of Evermore: Authorized Power Play Guide	$12.95
Secret of Mana Official Game Secrets	$14.95
Sega CD Official Game Secrets	$12.95
GamePro Presents: Sega Genesis Games Secrets Greatest Tips, Second Edition	$12.95
Official Sega Genesis Power Tips Book, Volumes 2, and 3	$14.95 each
Sega Genesis Secrets, Volume 4	$12.95
Sega Genesis and Sega CD Secrets, Volume 5	$12.95
Sega Genesis Secrets, Volume 6	$12.95
Sonic 3 Official Play Guide	$12.95
Super Empire Strikes Back Official Game Secrets	$12.95
Super Mario World Game Secrets	$12.95
Super Metroid Unauthorized Game Secrets	$14.95
Super NES Games Secrets, Volumes 2, and 3	$11.95 each
Super NES Games Secrets, Volumes 4 and 5	$12.95 each
GamePro Presents: Super NES Games Secrets Greatest Tips	$11.95
Super NES Games Unauthorized Power Tips Guide, Volumes 1 and 2	$14.95 each
Super Star Wars Official Game Secrets	$12.95
Urban Strike Official Power Play Guide, with Desert Strike & Jungle Strike	$12.95

TO ORDER BOOKS

Please send me the following items:

Quantity	Title	Unit Price	Total
______	______________________	$______	$______
______	______________________	$______	$______
______	______________________	$______	$______
______	______________________	$______	$______
______	______________________	$______	$______
______	______________________	$______	$______
		Subtotal	$______
		7.25% Sales Tax (CA only)	$______
		8.25% Sales Tax (TN only)	$______
		5.0% Sales Tax (MD only)	$______
		7.0% G.S.T. Canadian Orders	$______
		Shipping and Handling*	$______
		TOTAL ORDER	$______

*$4.00 shipping and handling charge for the first book, and $1.00 for each additional book.

By telephone: With Visa or MC, call 1-916-632-4400. Mon.–Fri. 9–4 PST. **By mail:** Just fill out the information below and send with your remittance to:

PRIMA PUBLISHING
P.O. Box 1260BK
Rocklin, CA 95677-1260

Satisfaction unconditionally guaranteed

Name______________________________________

Address____________________________________

City____________________ State__________ Zip__________

Visa /MC#__________________________ Exp.__________

Signature___________________________________